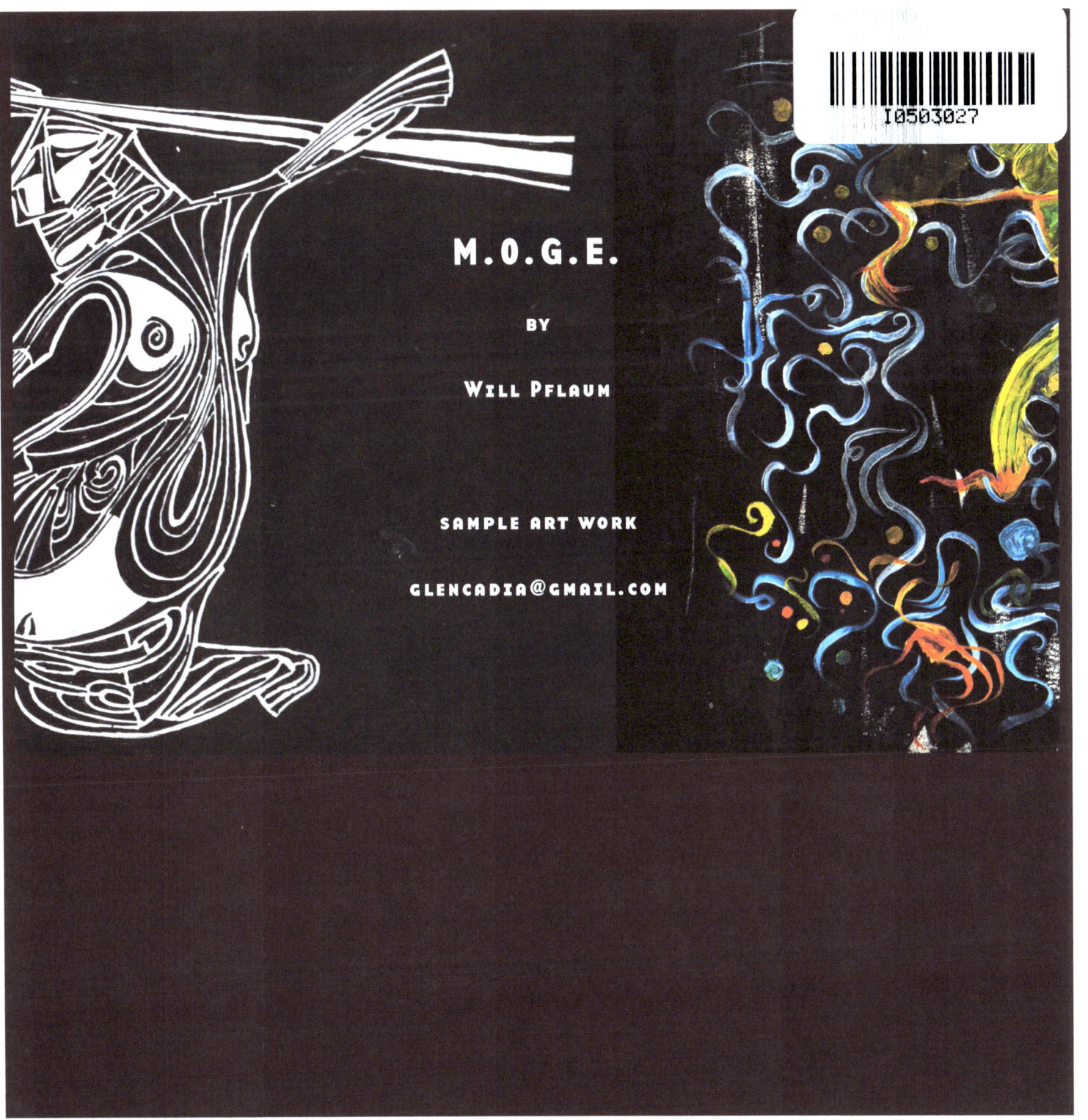

M.O.G.E.

BY

WILL PFLAUM

SAMPLE ART WORK

GLENCADIA@GMAIL.COM

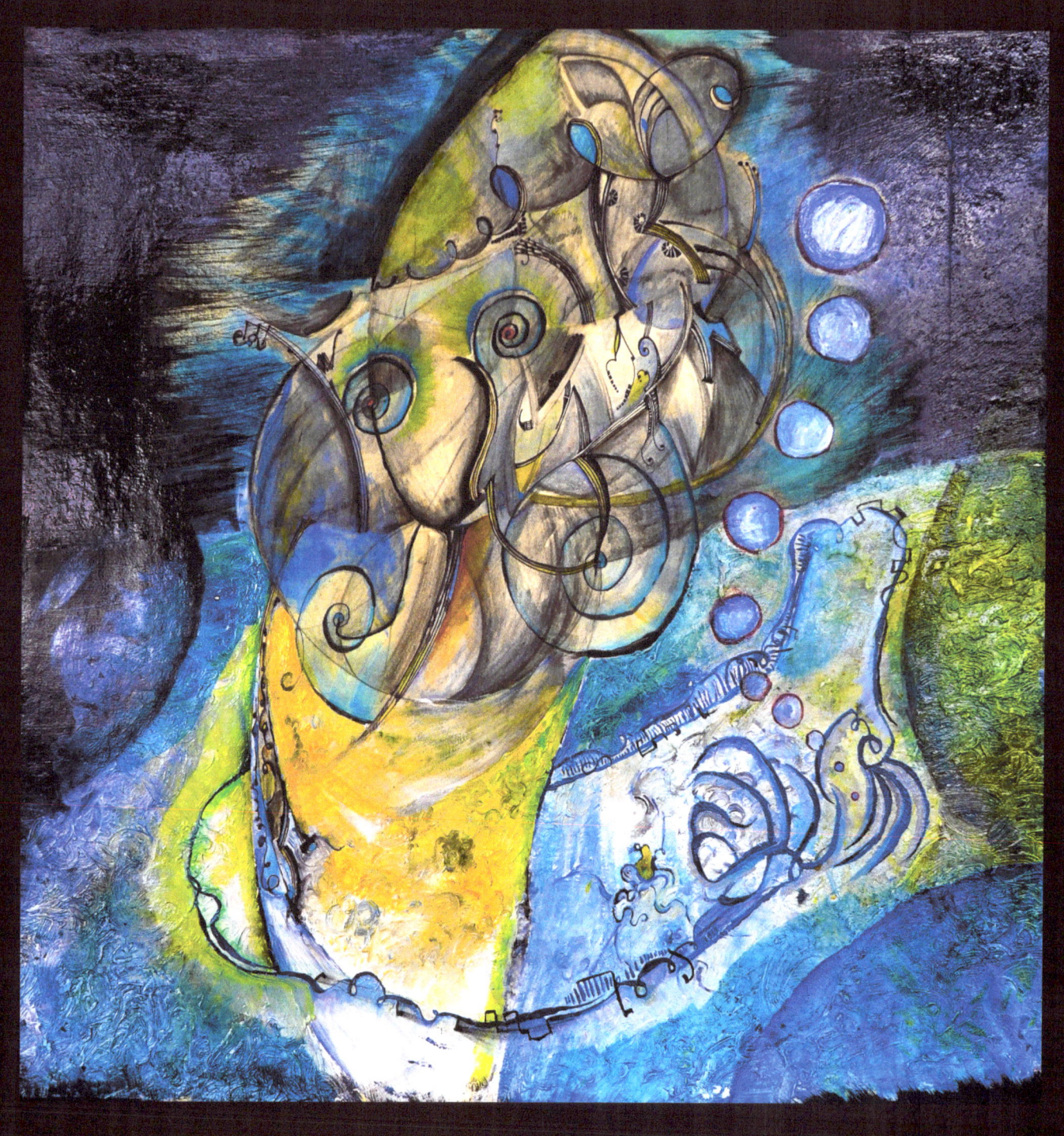

DISAPPOINTED 24X24" (61X61 CM), OIL, PENCIL, CHARCOL ON PAPER, 2012

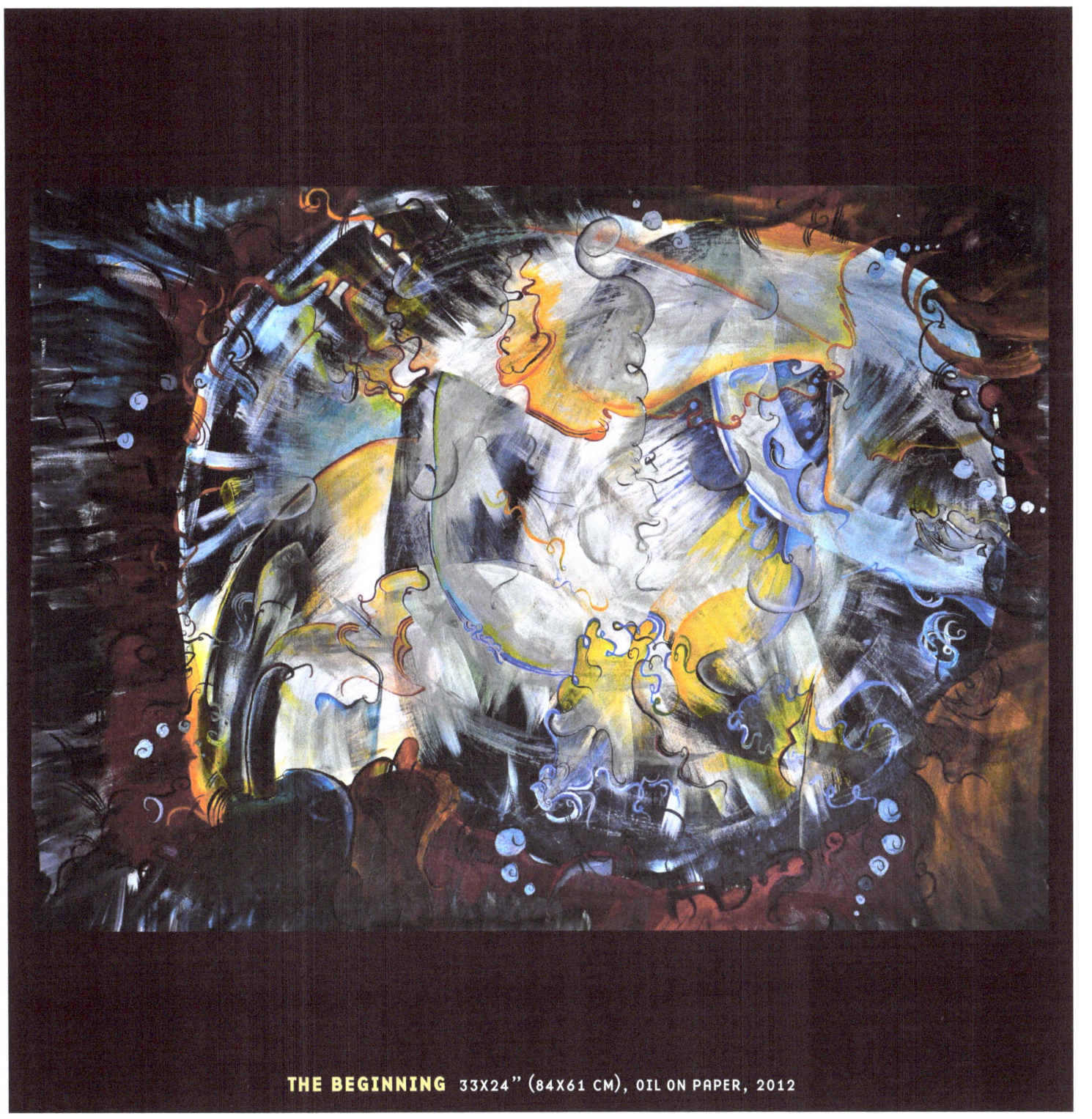

THE BEGINNING 33X24" (84X61 CM), OIL ON PAPER, 2012

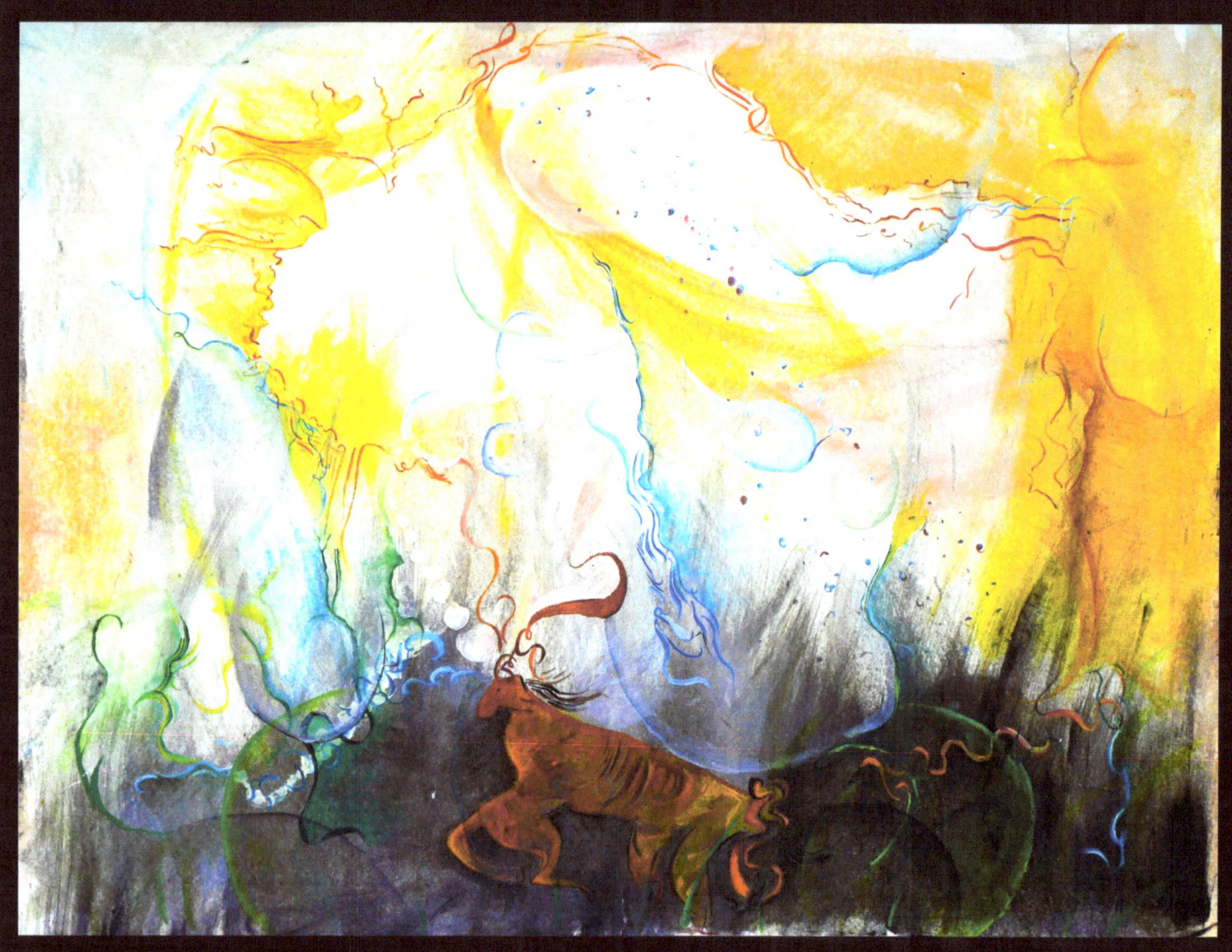

BEAST AMONG THE ELEMENTS 18X24" (46X61 CM), OIL ON PAPER, 2012

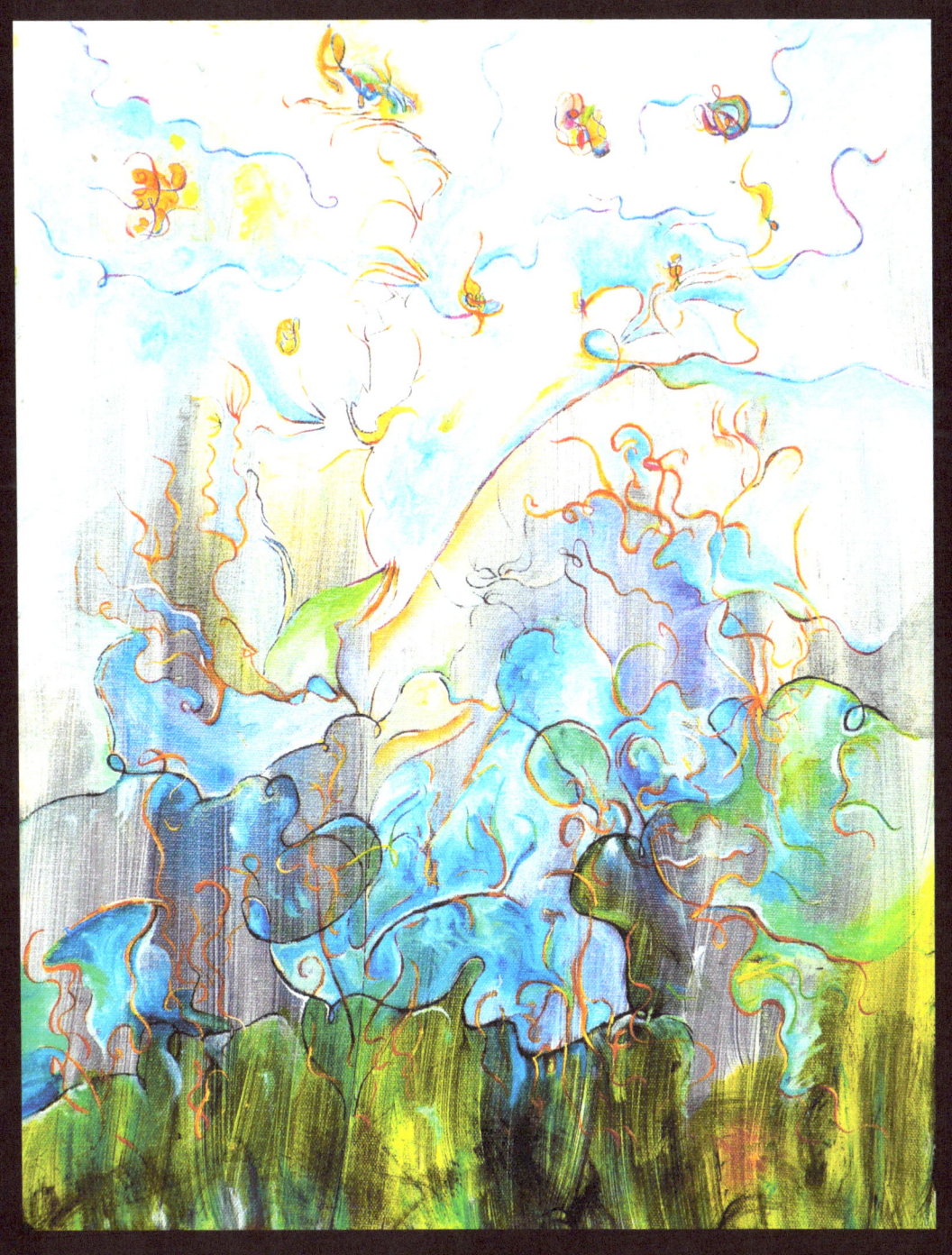

INEVITABLE BURSTING 18X24" (41X51 CM), OIL ON CANVAS, 2012

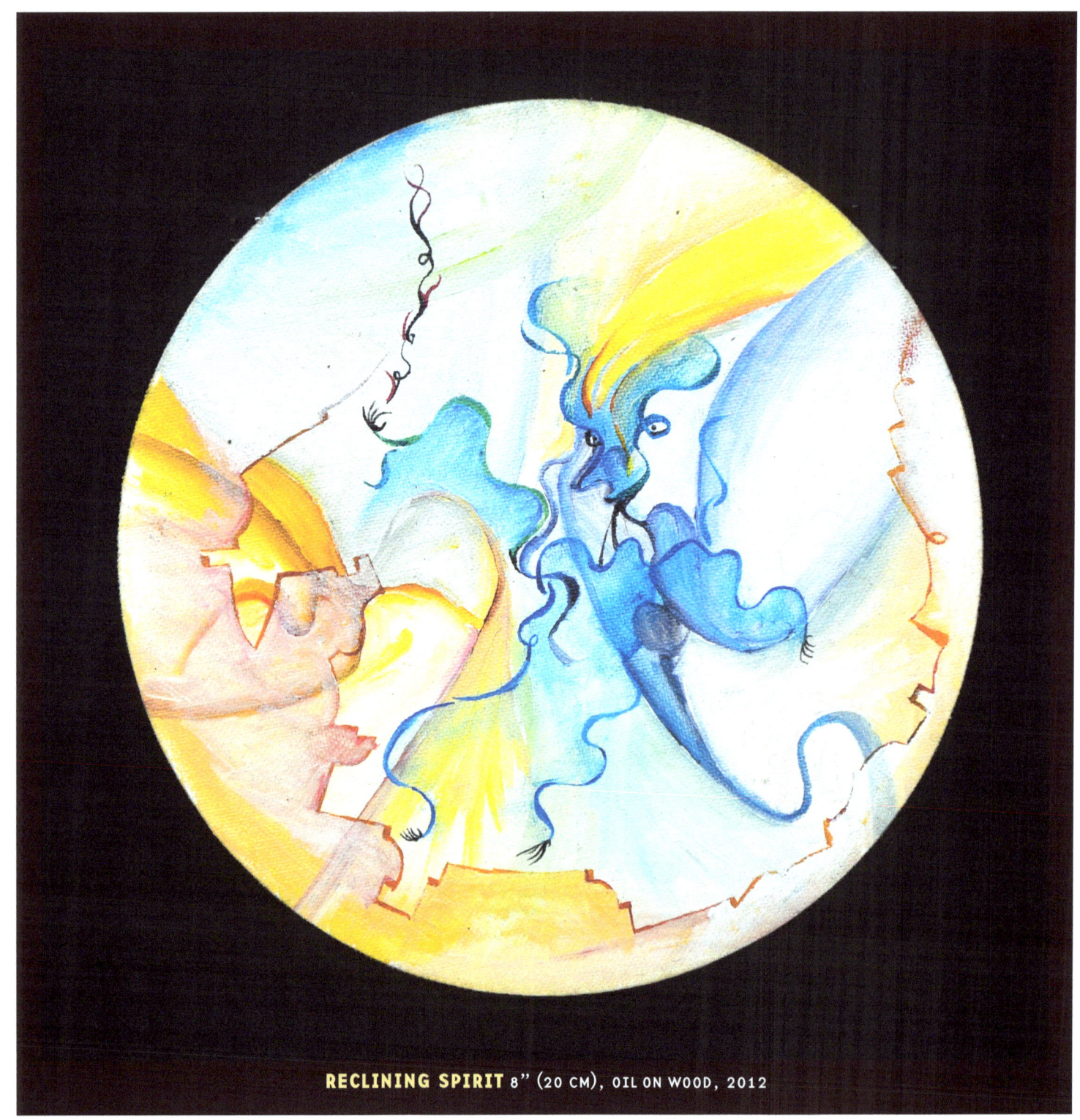

RECLINING SPIRIT 8" (20 CM), OIL ON WOOD, 2012

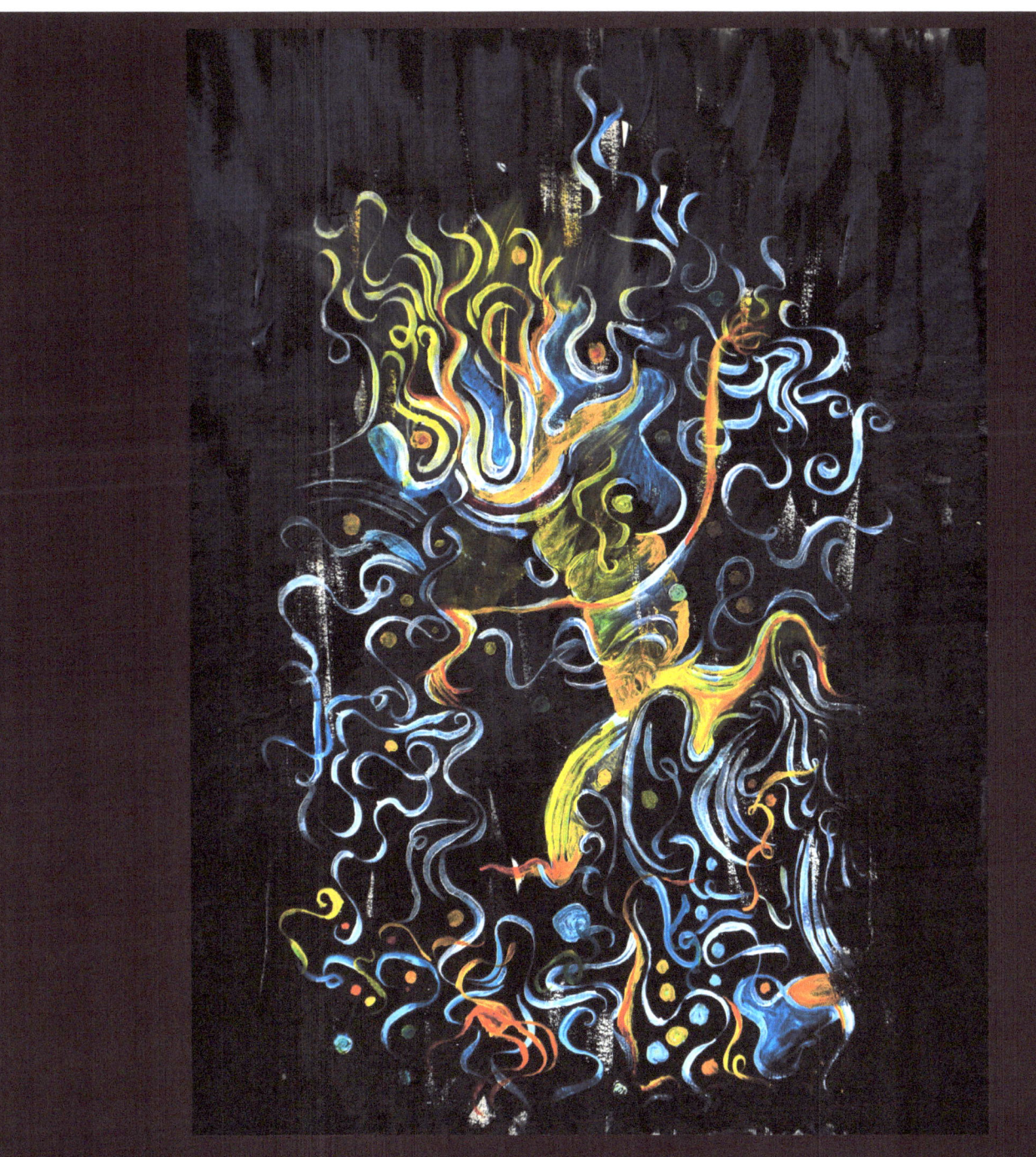

FIRE SPIRIT 15X20" (38X51 CM), OIL ON PAPER, 2012

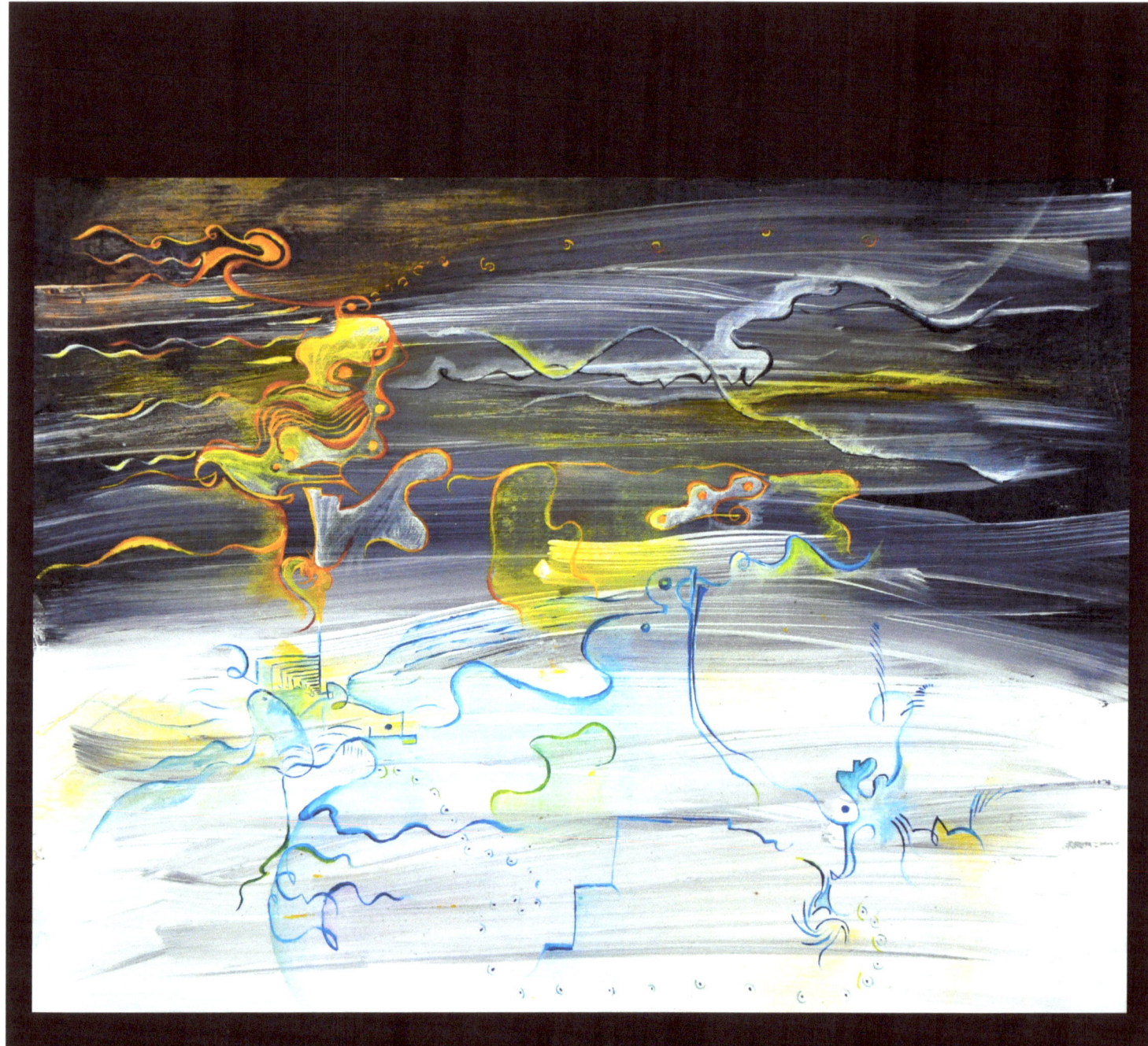

NIGHT AT SEA 16X12" (41X30 CM), OIL ON CANVAS, 2012

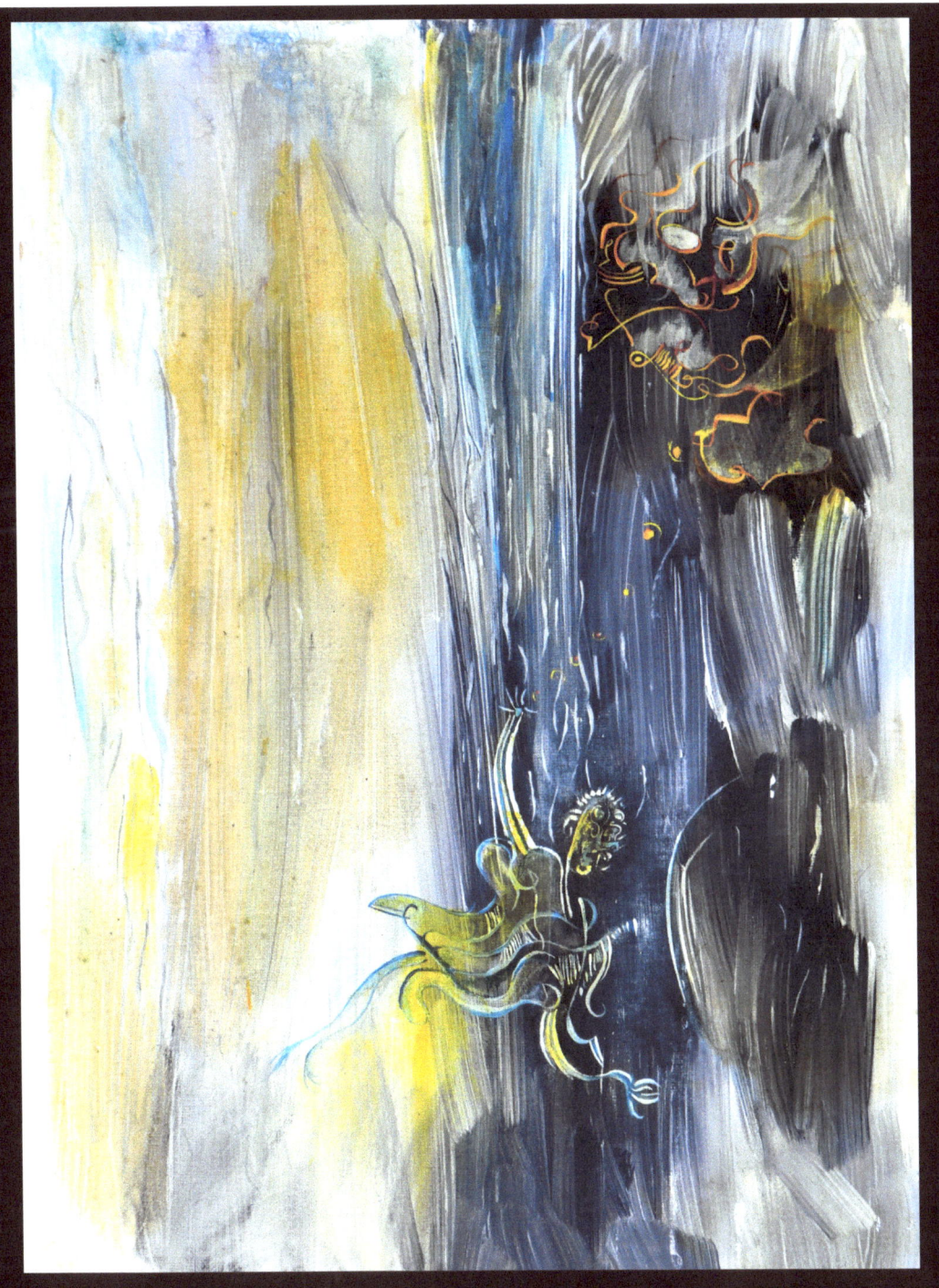

NIGHT AT SEA 16X12" (41X30 CM), OIL ON CANVAS, 2012

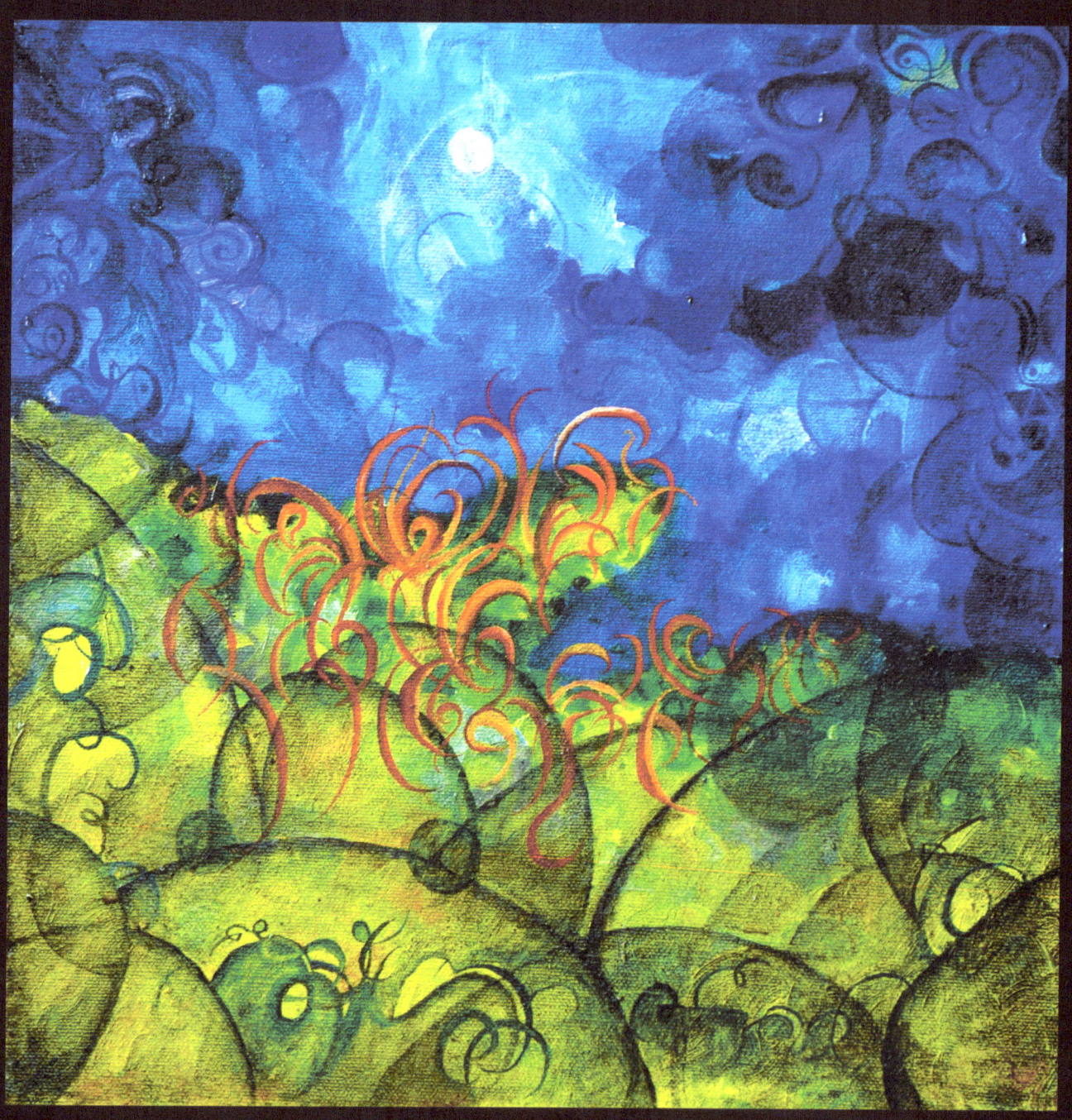

MOON ON CANE 12X12" (30X30 CM), OIL ON CANVAS, 2002

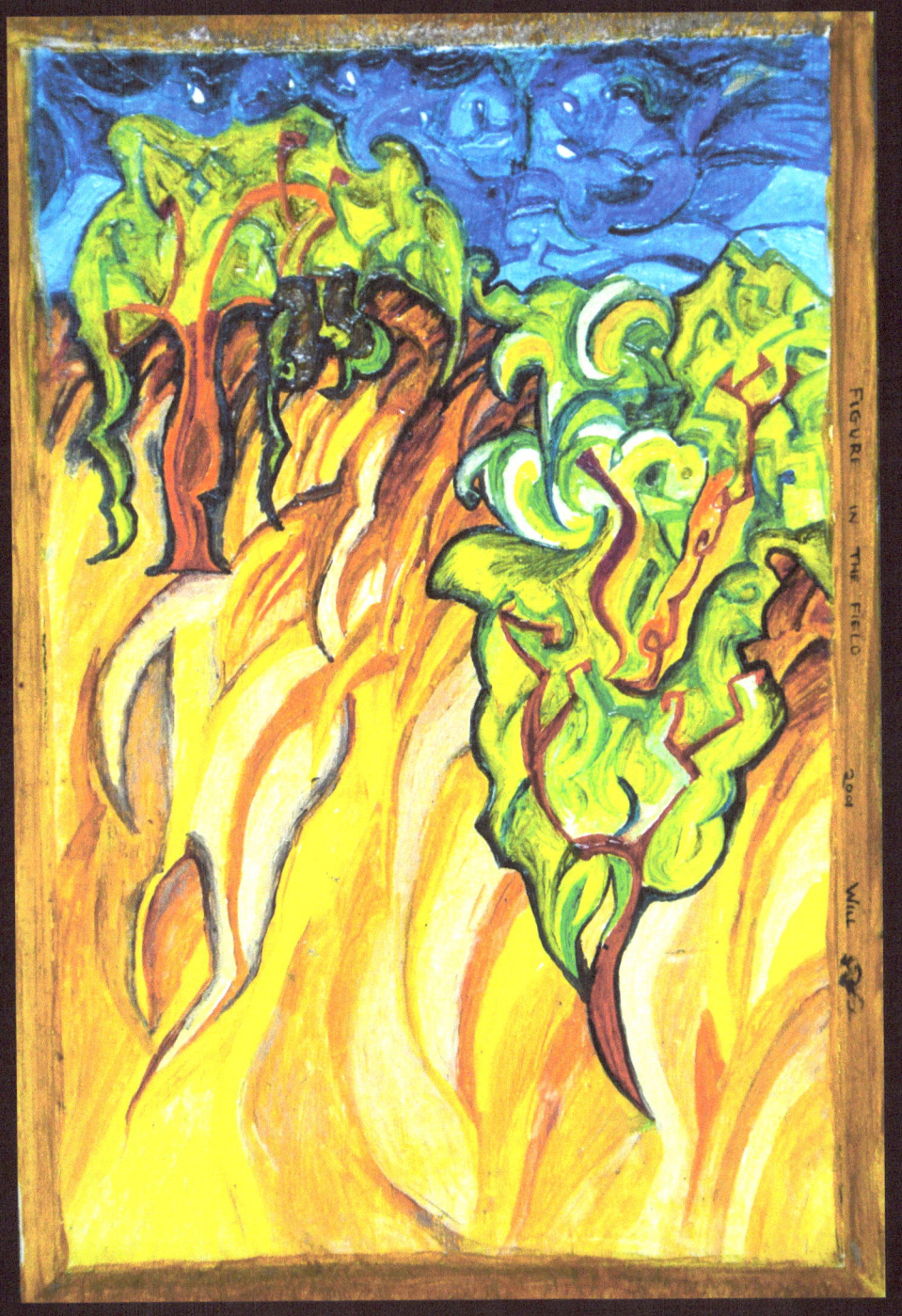

FIGURE IN THE FIELD 6.5X9.5" (17X24 CM), OIL ON WOOD, 2002

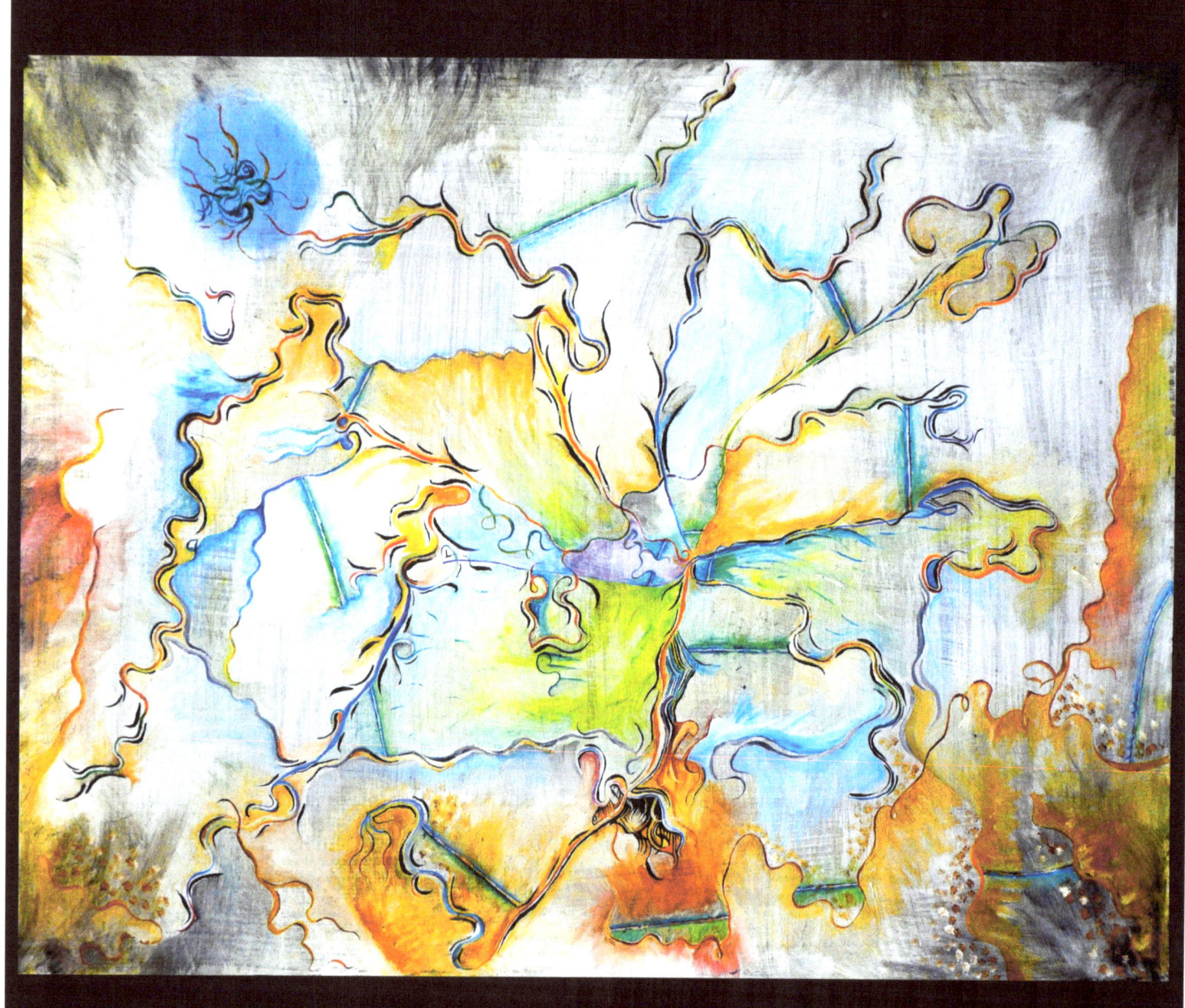

BUTTERFLY, FLOWER AND RAINBOW STEMS 22X17.5" (56X45 CM), OIL ON WOOD, 2012

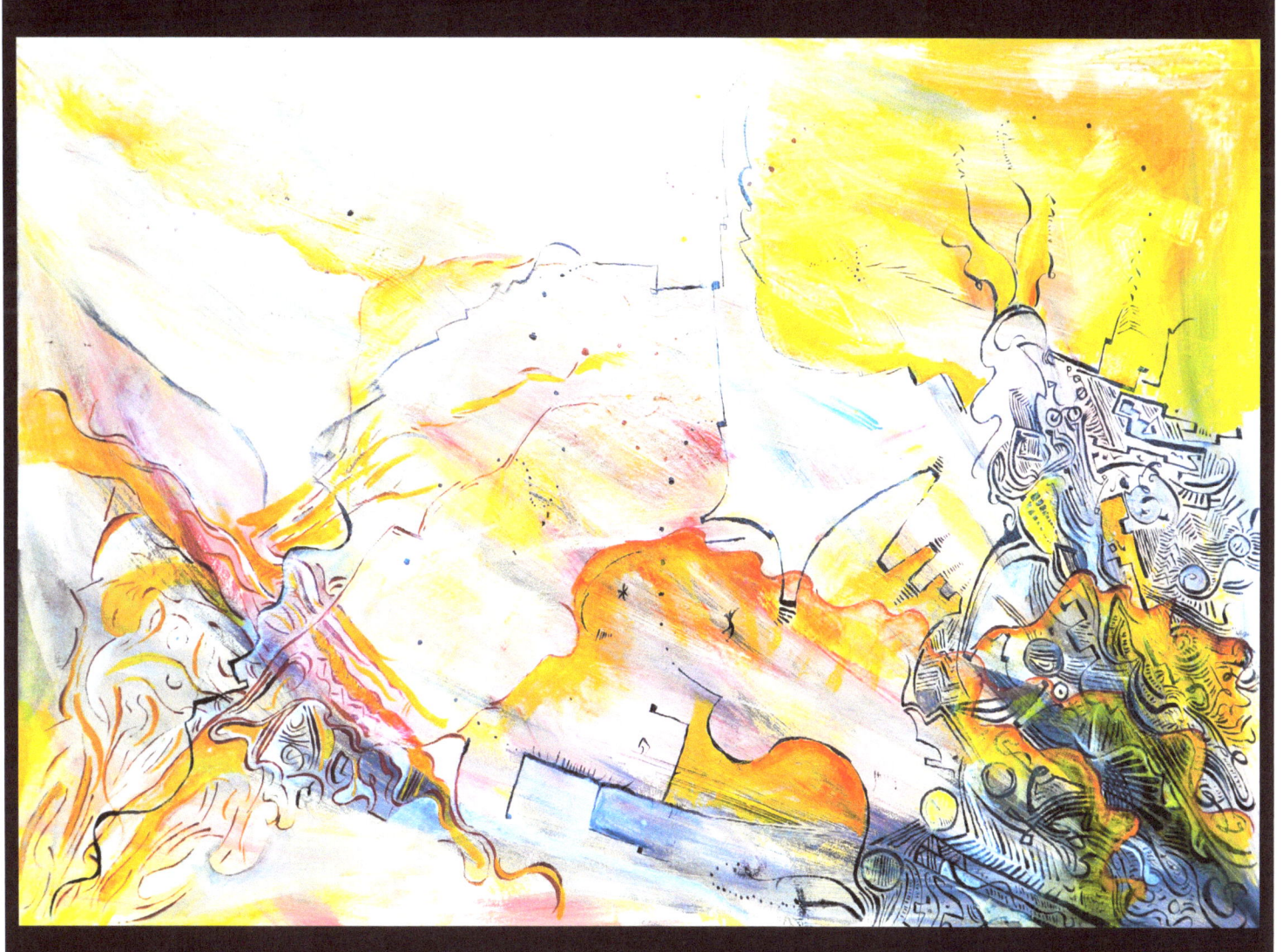

PINK CATAPULT 18X12" (30X46 CM), OIL ON PAPER, 2012

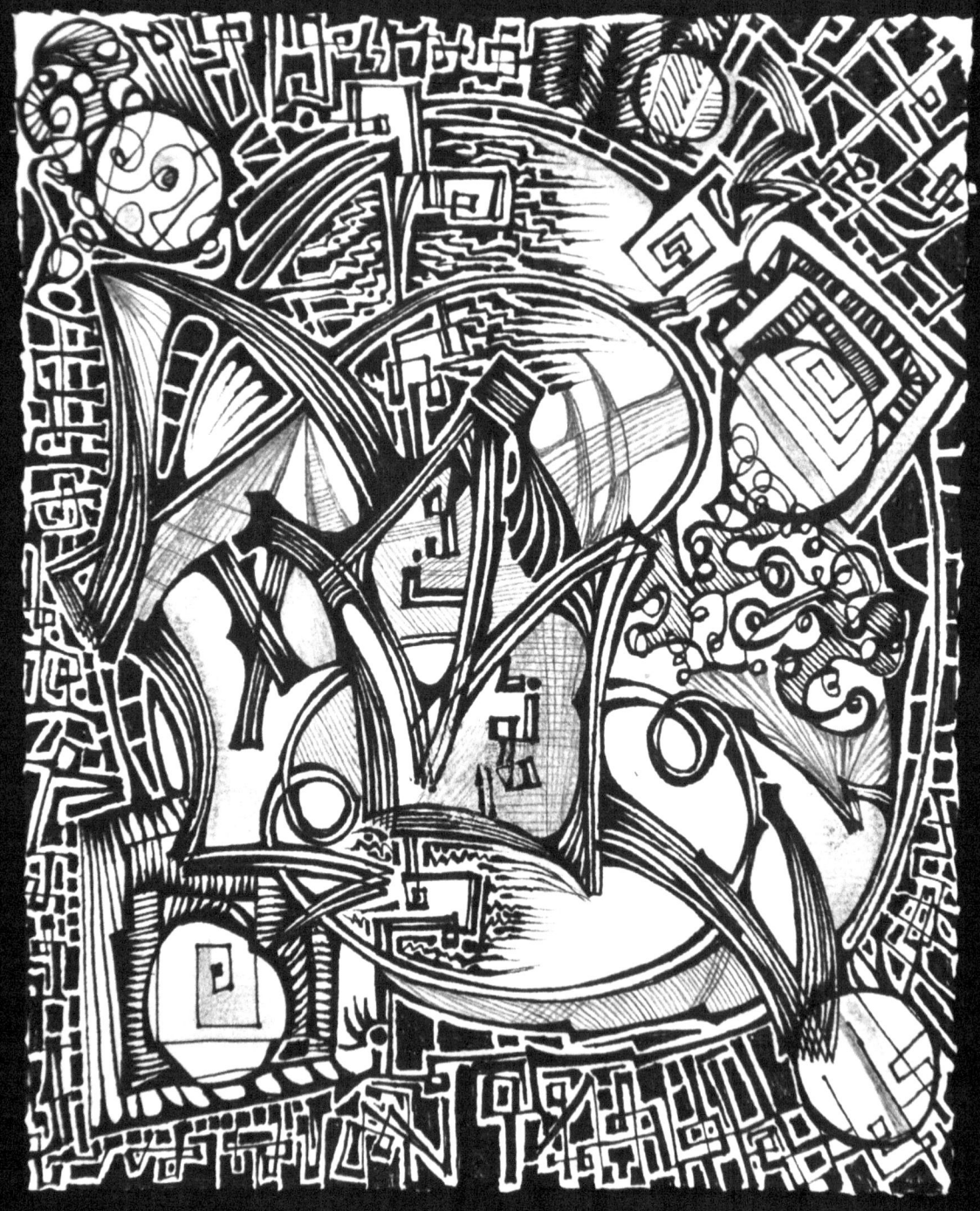

NETTED 7.5X8.5" (19X22 CM), INK ON PAPER, 2004

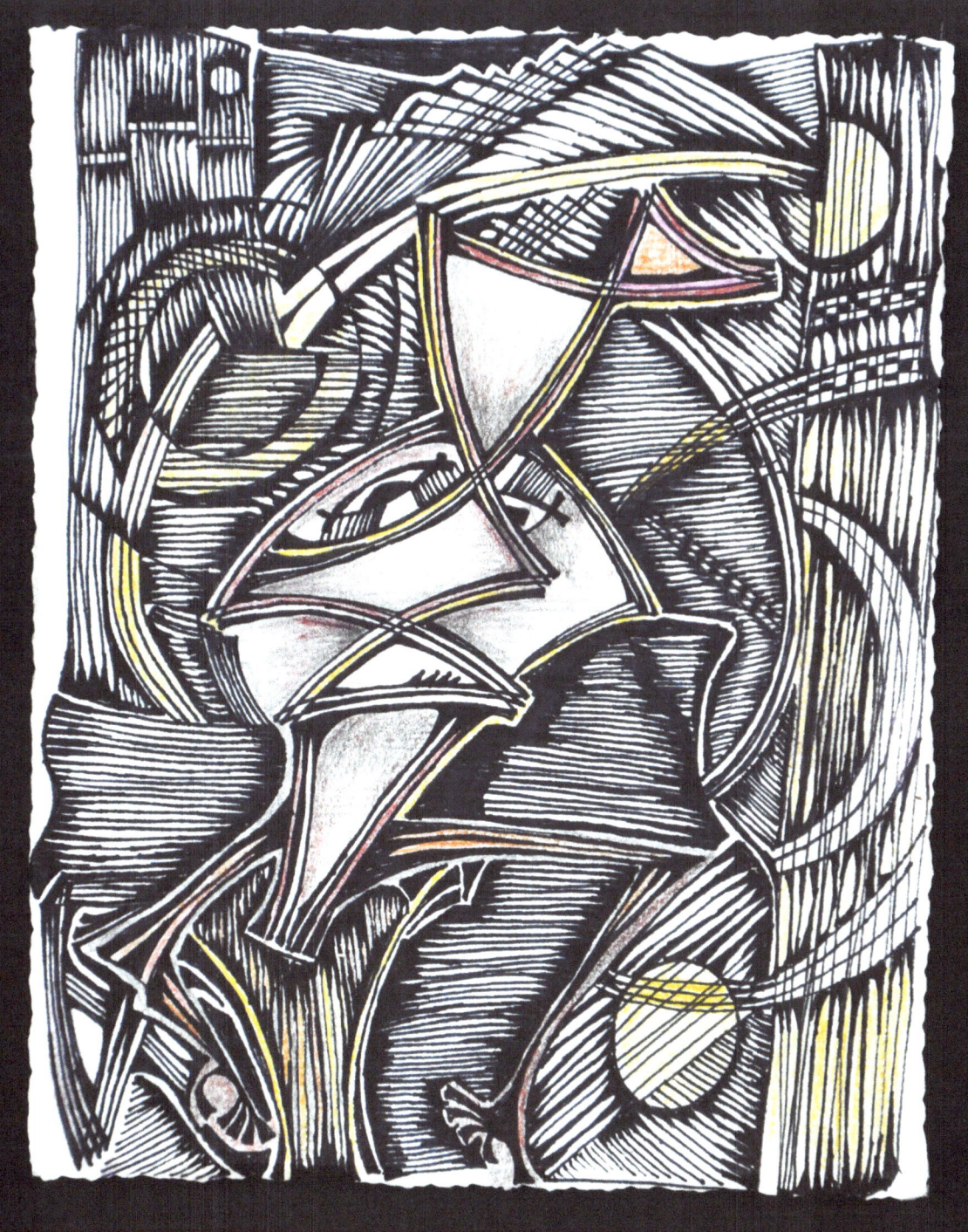

UNFORTUNATELY EMBEDDED 7.5X8.5" (19X22 CM), INK AND WATERCOLOR ON PAPER, 2004

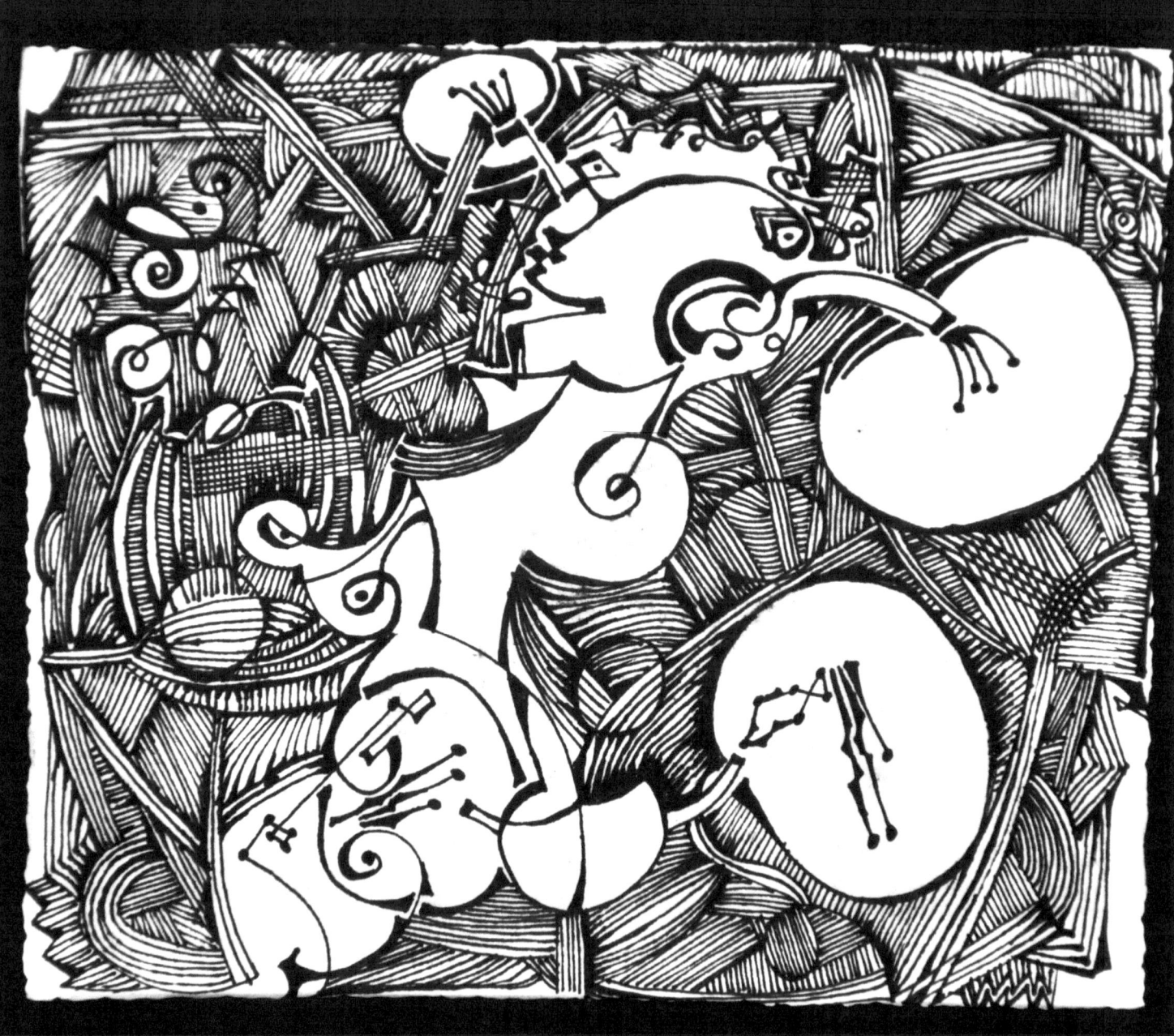

DELIGHTED BY BUBBLES 8.5X7.5" (22X19 CM), INK ON PAPER, 2004

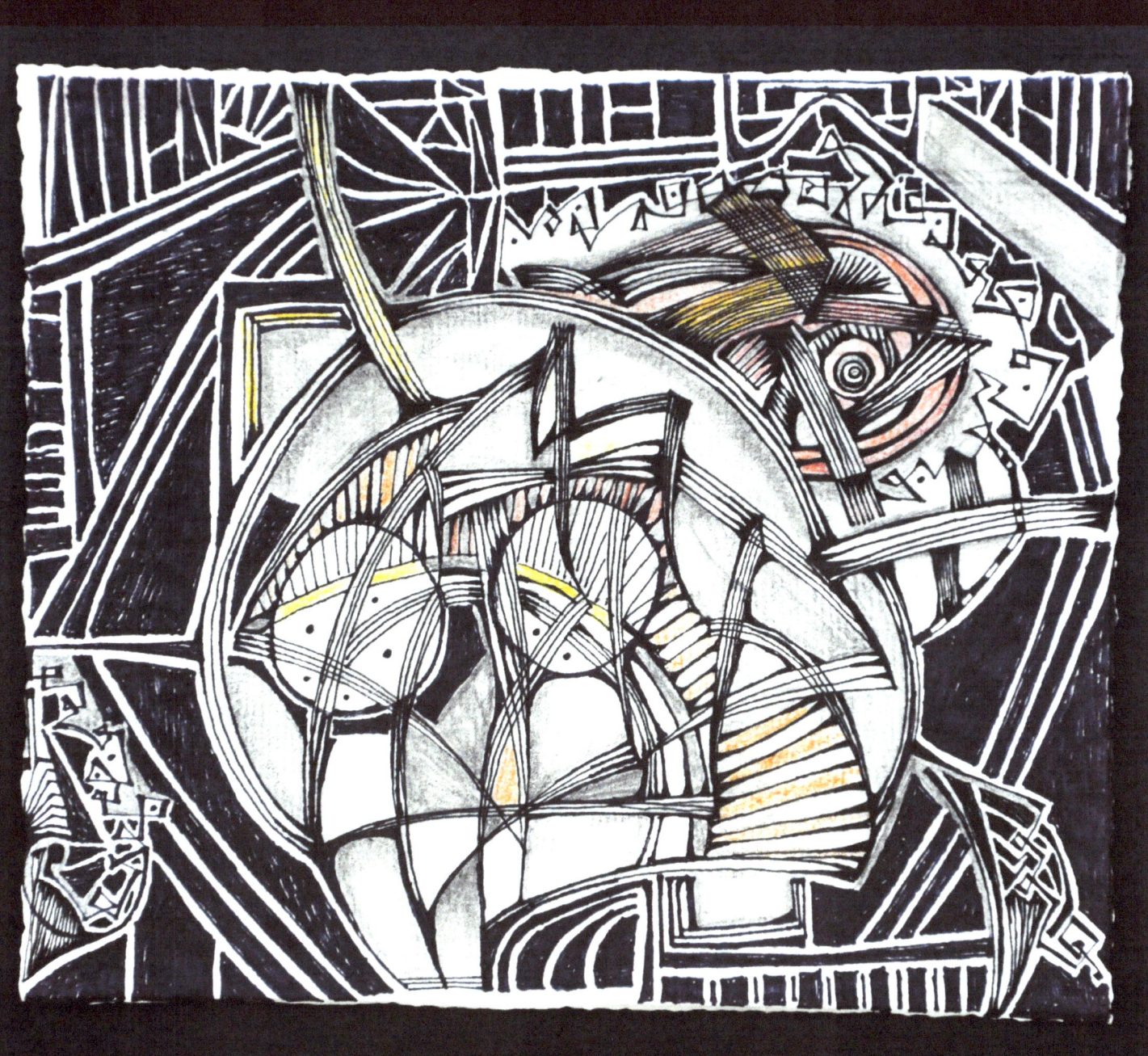

EYES OF THE HUNGRY CROW 8.5X7.5" (22X19 CM), INK AND WATERCOLOR ON PAPER, 2004

PIECES

Her wind in sand dunes
Making patterns,
Or in collisions in space,
Her breath never ceases.

She brings order
To the cells of your body
And to Saturn's rings.

She whispers desire to
All discrete pieces.

You cannot pray to this goddess
Or write her a scripture
But if you have lusted
She is there when you sing.

The goddess does not love us:
Blood on the altar,
Flesh in her fire.

Her force in our art,
The goddess lies to us less
Than the war god of Israel,
Yahweh, God the Father,
True liar.

Order from chaos through Eros,
Particles in streams combine,
And so we live.

Fear the fierce goddess,
Cruel, she is.
But life she gives.

PORN WON'T READ THIS

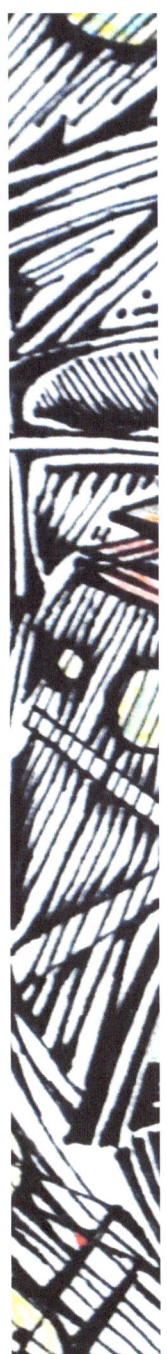

Cause of death: overdose
On Vieux Boulogne cheese
While screwing a skunk
During a heat wave in August.
This poem died and should have stunk
Like a sheep shit pellet.
Hell it should reek until it
Develops a funky cloud,
A stink that envelops
Producing hives and welps
and welts, a rash on the skin,
Leaving your nostrils torn.
Then along came Porn.
He walked on by
And couldn't smell it.

Porn is to this poem
As the universe is to
The vague hint of a thought
A flash in the eye
Concerning the idea of learning
Of the nonexistence
Of this very instance
In the absent inane brain
That cannot indeed think or talk
As the non-brain is not,
As it is in an inanimate object,
Like a rock.

This poem, so damn dead and smelly,
Lives in a cardboard shanty
Inside the sewage treatment plant
In New Delhi.
The poem won't eat today.
It's dead. It can't.

Porn's has a private jet, of course.
If this poem had a horse
It would eat it.
Infinite porn in every pocket
And an infinite number of poems
But you forgot that.
Should I repeat it?

Download a poem app?
I thought not.
I think not.
I sink into you and stink not.
I feel every inch of your skin
And get caught.
Because I have time.
And your warm touch
Is the only thing on my mind.

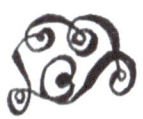

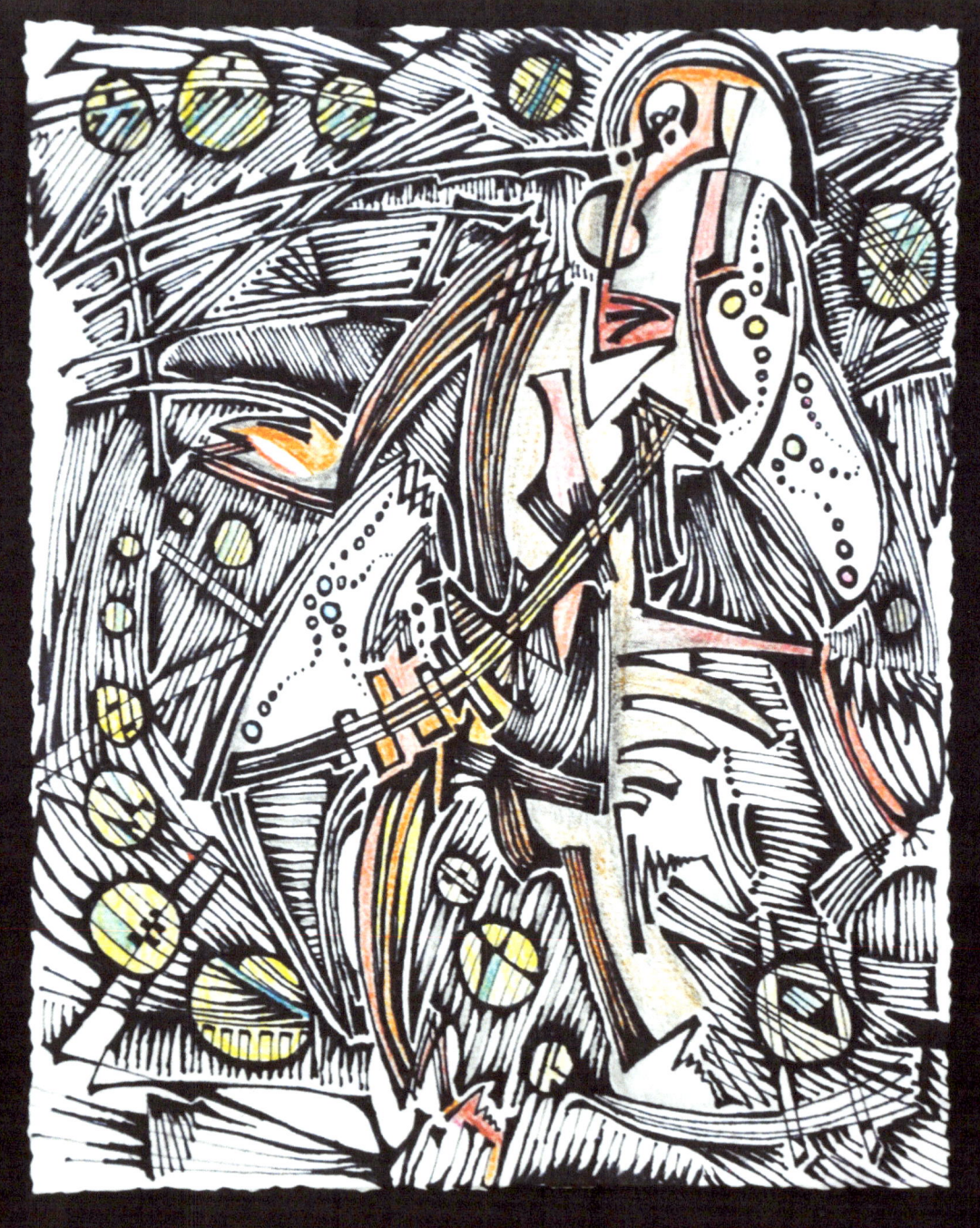

CONSIDERING THE WAY OUT 7.5X8.5" (19X22 CM), INK AND WATERCOLOR ON PAPER, 2004

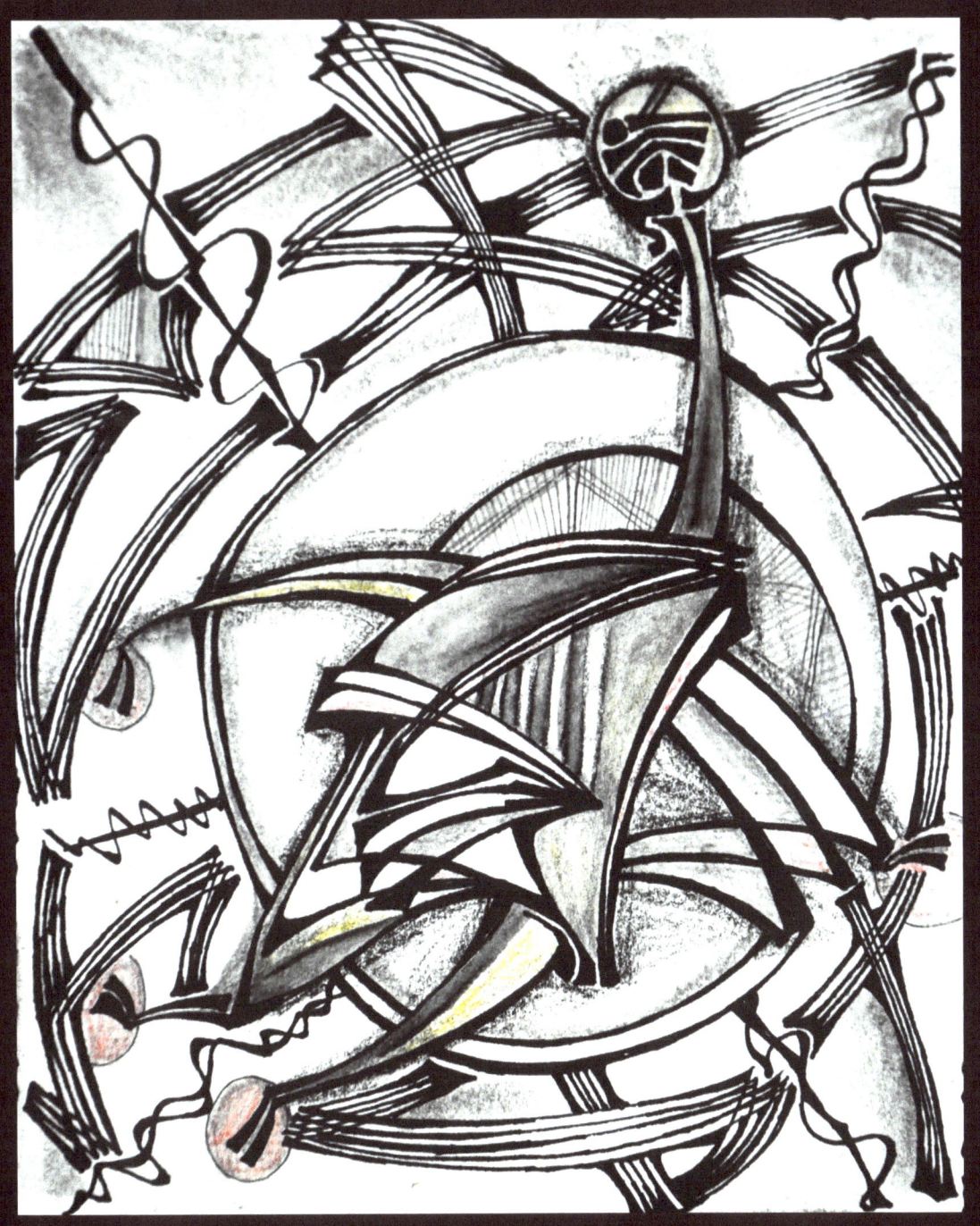

RECLINING SKELETON 7.5X8.5" (19X22 CM), INK, CHARCOL AND WATERCOLOR ON PAPER, 2004

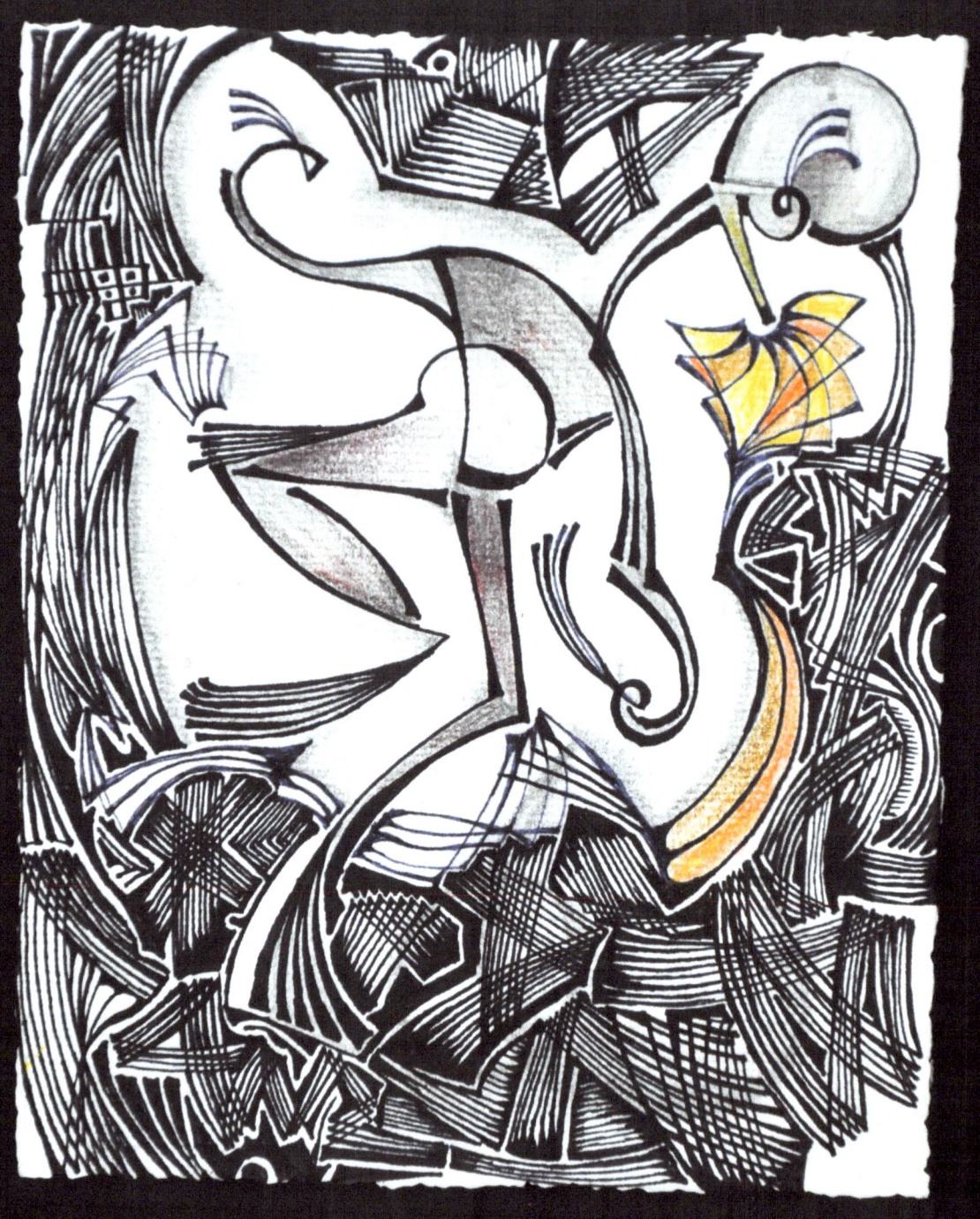

WATER CREATURE SMELLS A FLOWER 7.5X8.5" (19X22 CM), INK, CHARCOL AND WATERCOLOR ON PAPER, 2004

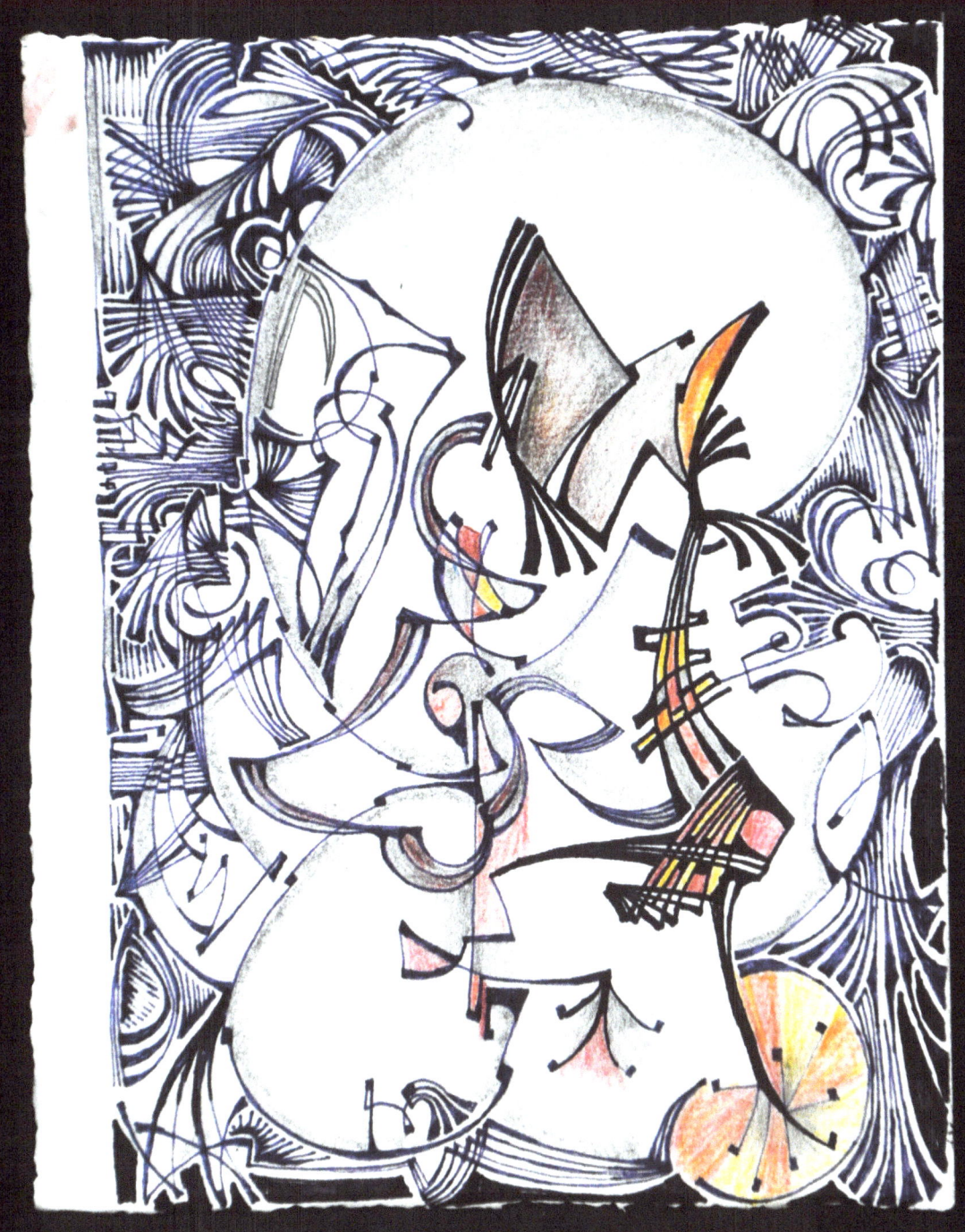

ROBOT SMELLS A FLOWER 7.5X8.5" (19X22 CM), INK, CHARCOL AND WATERCOLOR ON PAPER, 2004

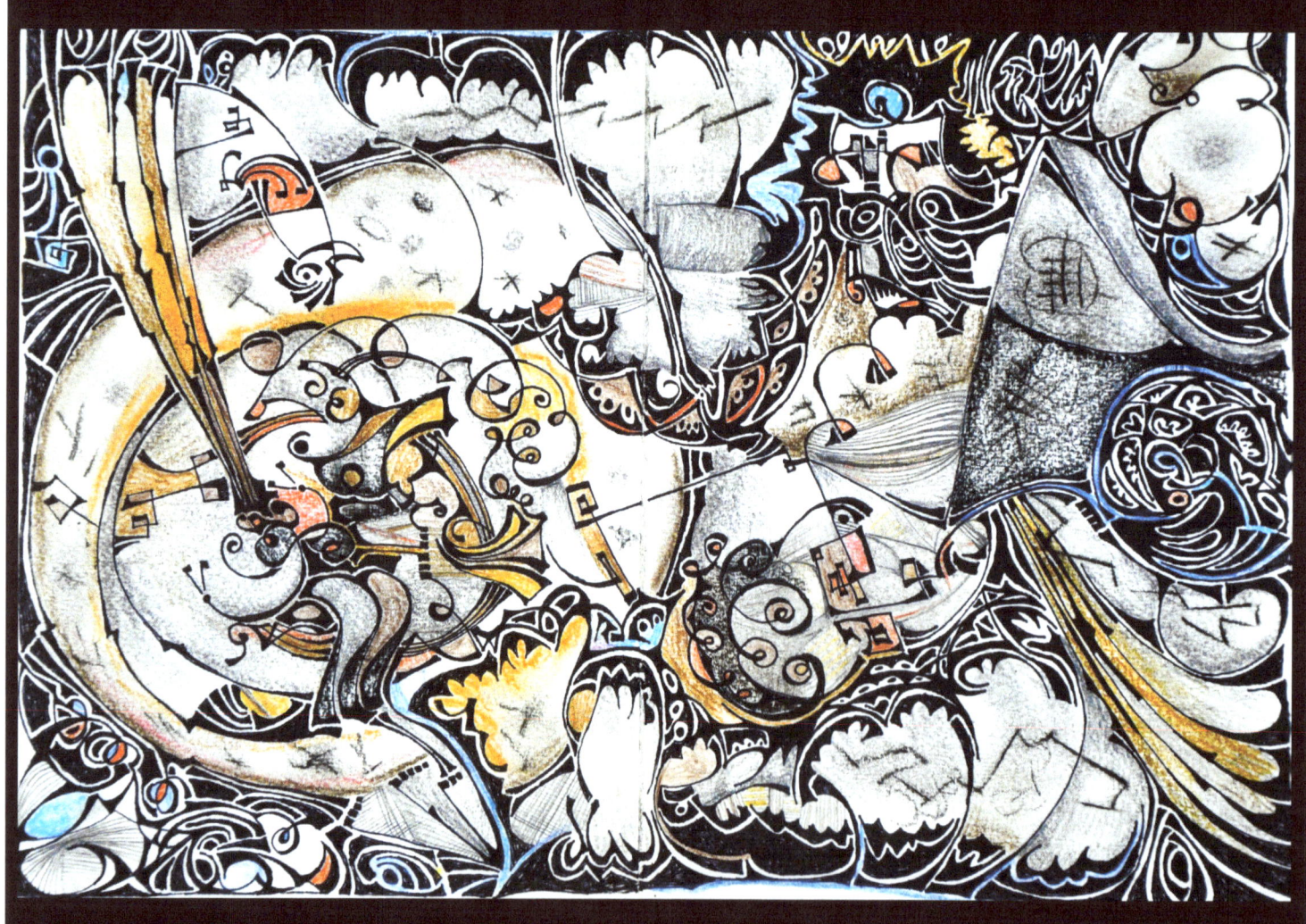

EMERGING ORDER 7.5X8.5" (19X22 CM), INK, PENCIL, CHARCOL AND WATERCOLOR ON PAPER, 2003

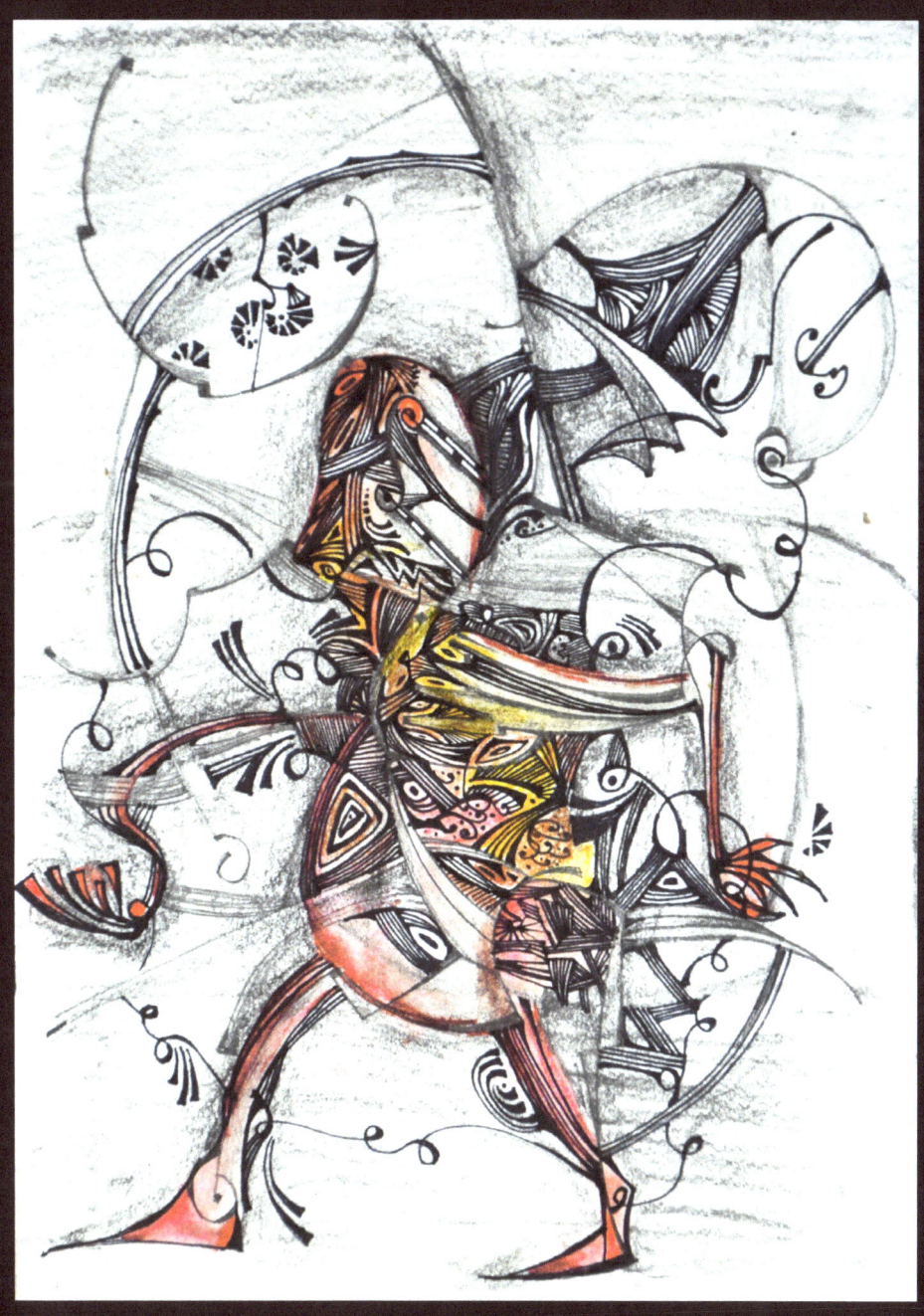

WALKING FIGURE 8X11" (20X28 CM), INK, PENCIL, AND CHARCOL ON PAPER, 2012

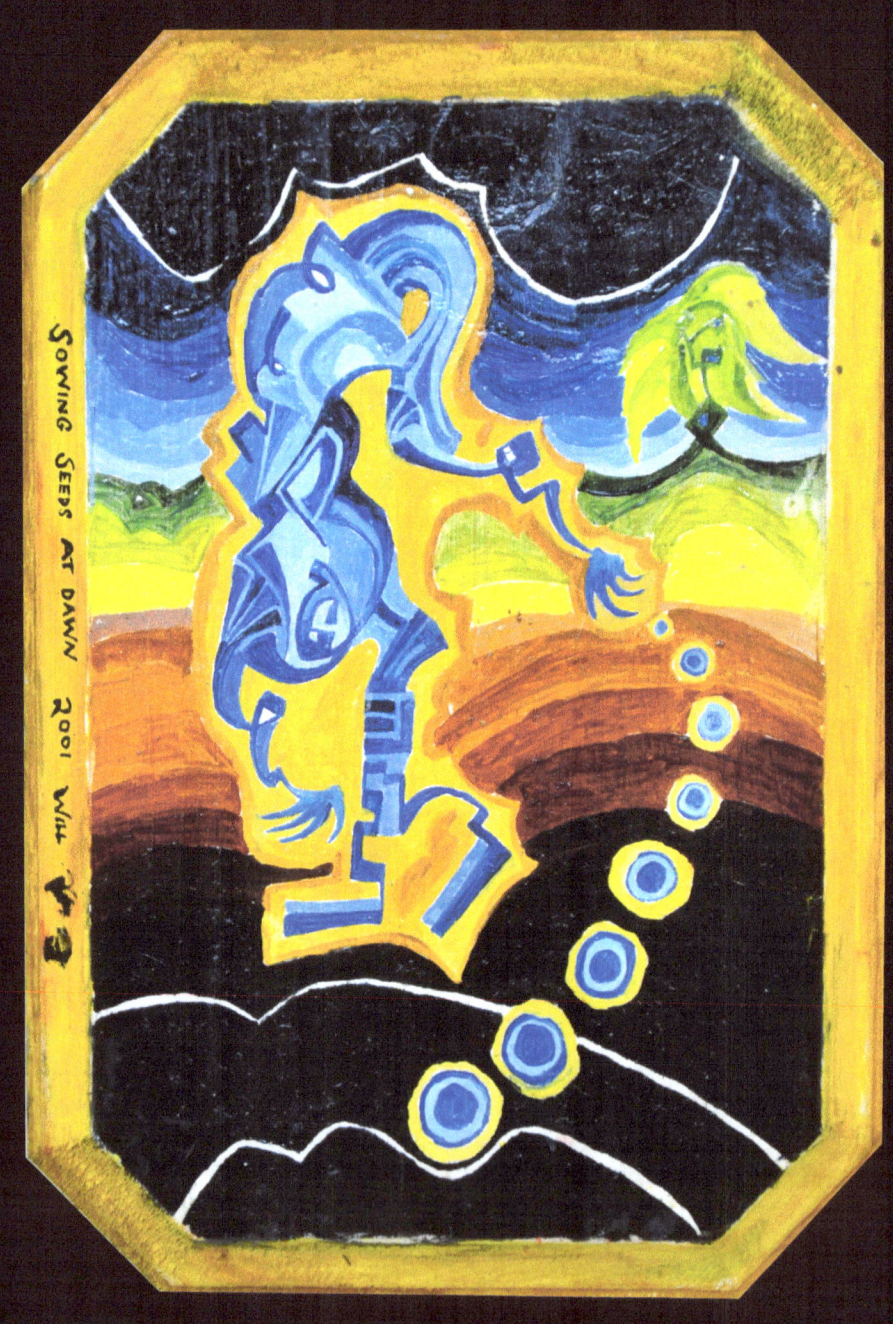

SOWING SEEDS AT DAWN 4.5X6.5" (11X16 CM), OIL ON WOOD, 2001

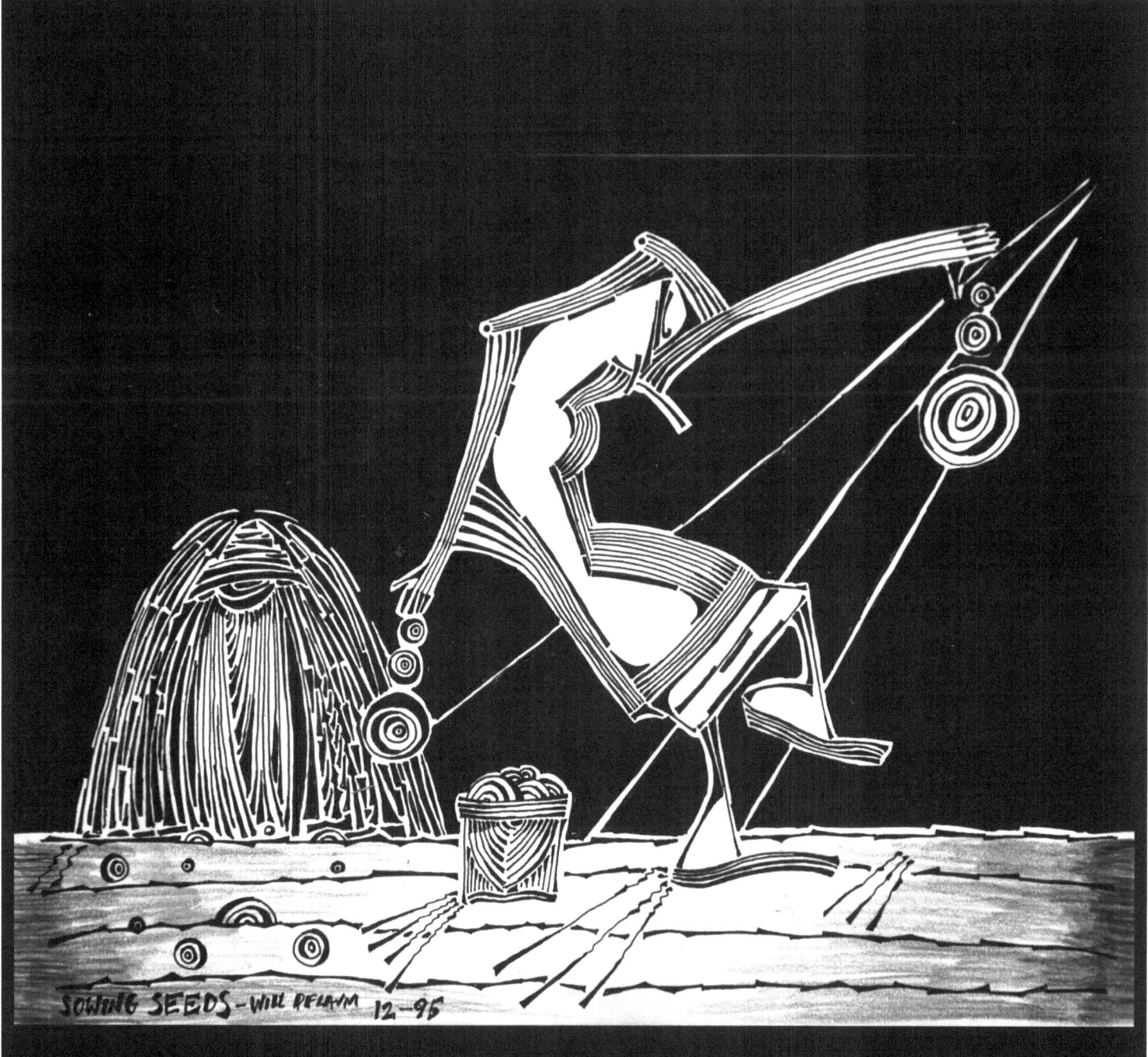

SOWING SEEDS 9X12" (23X30 CM), INK ON PAPER, 1995

WIND

Desire, like wind, blows, closing in, close enough,
Blowing the roof off your house
And ruining stuff.

On a colder day, when more wind came,
Or in a storm or rain,
Shouldn't puff that way
And blow away
Trees and things
But it does
Just because.

You might like to turn it down, any excess,
And resume all your other interests.

But wind can be useful to grind corn in windmills
And sail ships to America and discover that.
Without desire you'd be living in a flat.
Imagine the rent in London,
With everyone from Rio to LA
Trying to find a place to stay.

Eros, breath,
As if she sang it,
Chewing on the microphone
Or in pastel paint

On my brush,
Choosing pink.
Whiskey doesn't shake it off.
Drink, I let desire blow through me
And if you ask, I'll say, who me?

You'll find me in breezes,
In whirlwinds in corners,
And all other places
Always unexpressed
Seeing her face in a song,
Obsessed like this, I'm never wrong.
Trade winds, on a hill
The island is smiling,
Through the years and venues
To be like a sailboat and use this,
Because desire continues
And her eyes are grey like
The dust and mist at dawn
Obscuring the daylight.

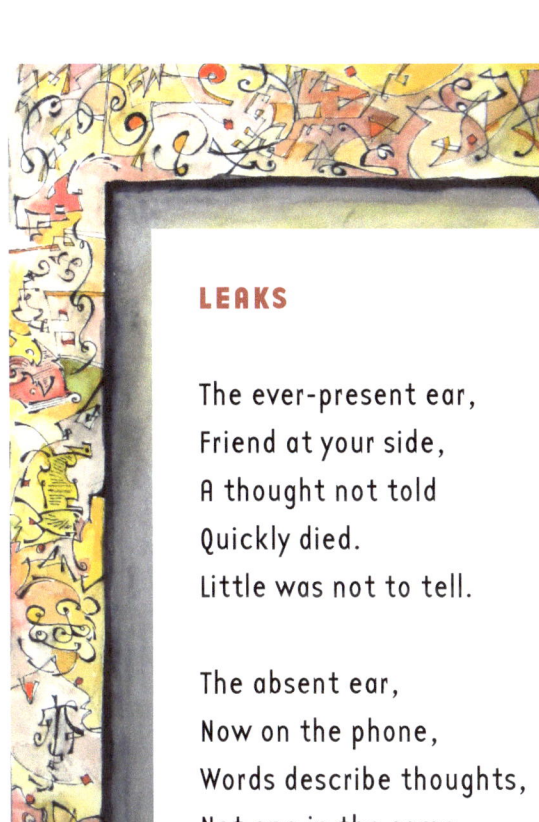

LEAKS

The ever-present ear,
Friend at your side,
A thought not told
Quickly died.
Little was not to tell.

The absent ear,
Now on the phone,
Words describe thoughts,
Not one in the same,
But the words did well.

The non-existent ear,
After so much time,
In a maturely, rigid mind,
Leaves thoughts to swirl unsaid
In their own wake propelled.

Wise is the revealing the child,
Sloppily loving friends with graceless ability.
Cannibal concepts make water wild,
As you age into careful, quiet, lonely imbecility.

Head of household, a storm of thoughts,
But not a word will speak.
Chatting, careful, guarded,
So no drop of raining dream can leak.

Not a wisp or mist or hint,
No one will detect
Any stupid notion
And your ridiculous emotion.

A leak would endanger your position.
Or maybe you just forgot
How to love a friend
But twenty years ago
This was not how
It was supposed to end.

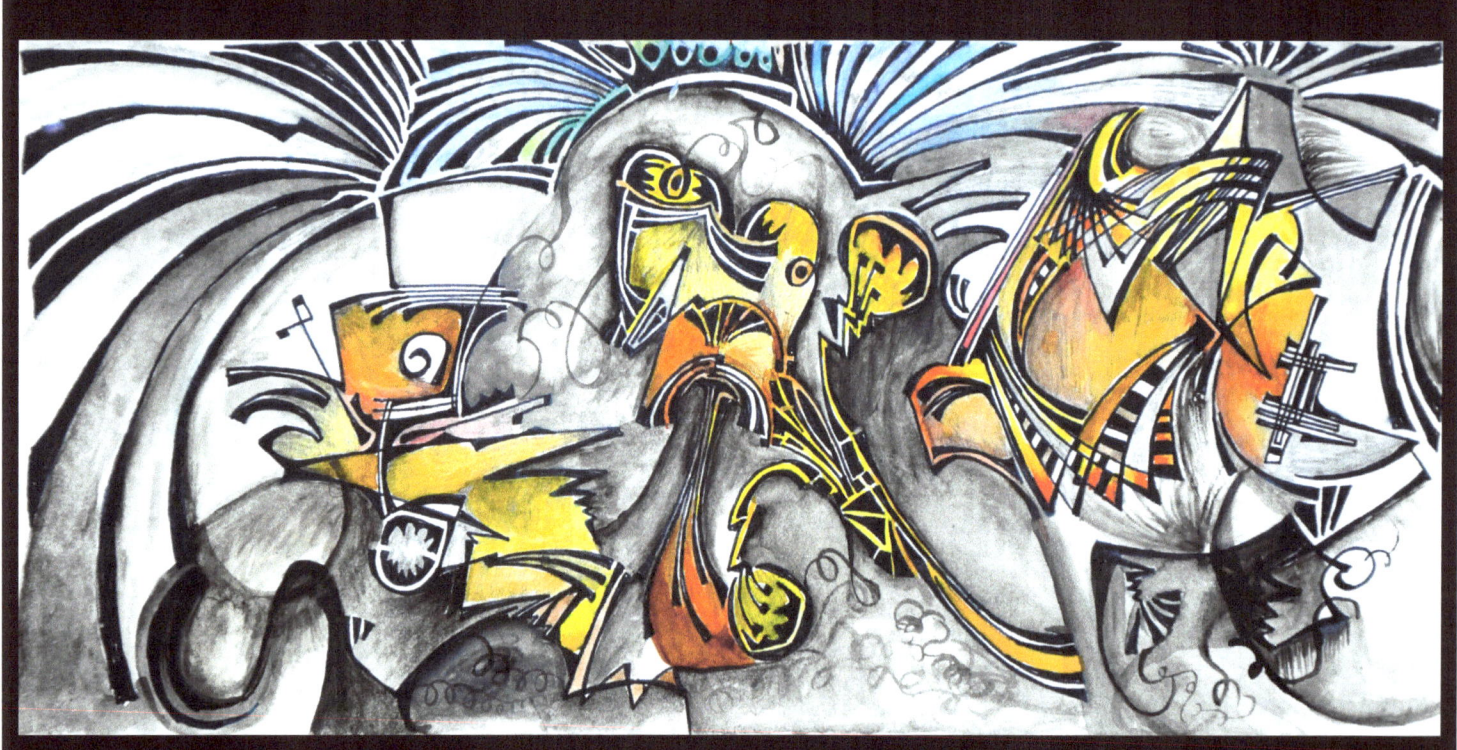

FIERCE TOLTEC GODS 7X20" (18X51 CM), INK, PENCIL AND WATERCOLOR ON PAPER, 1998

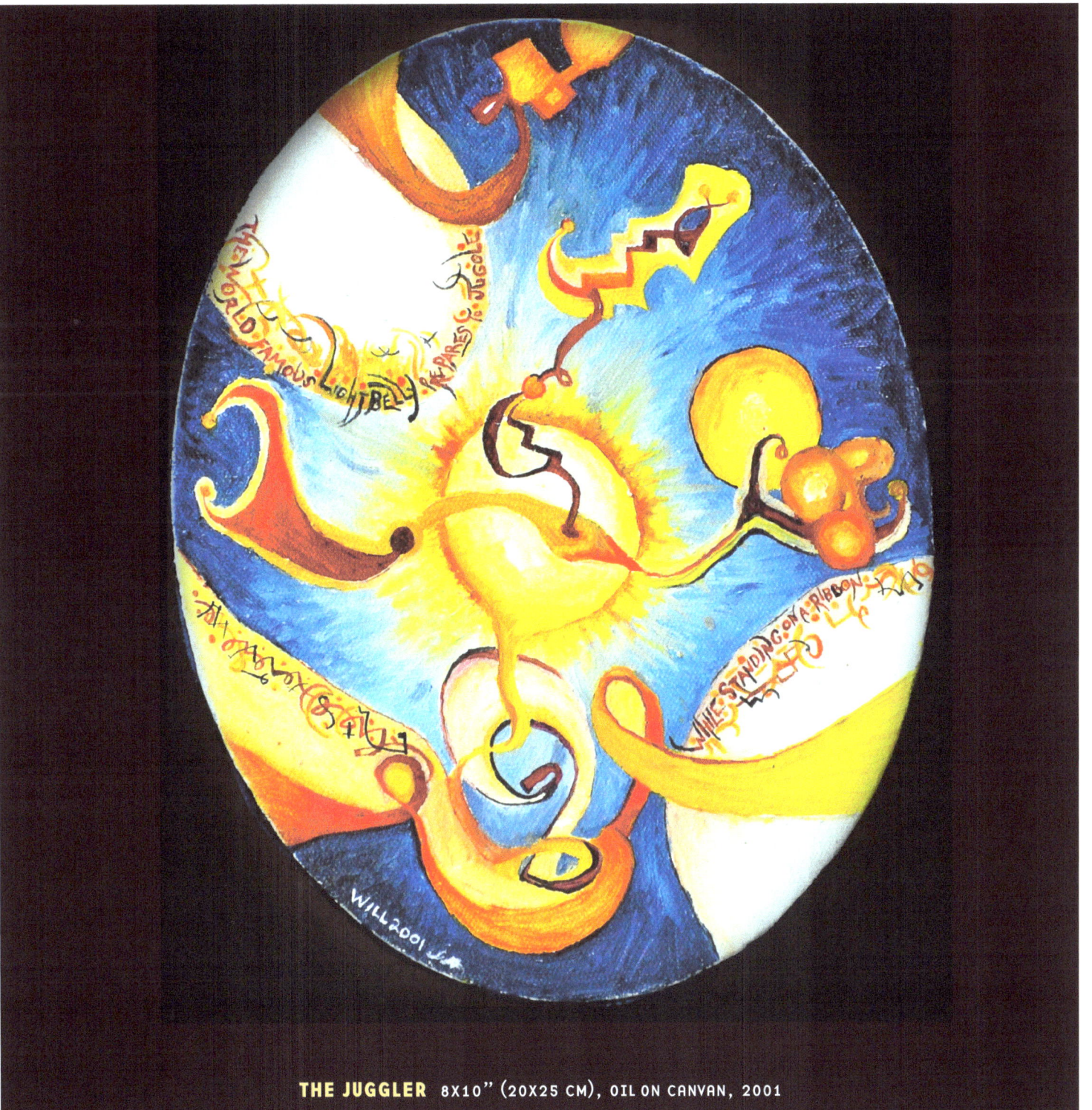

THE JUGGLER 8X10" (20X25 CM), OIL ON CANVAN, 2001

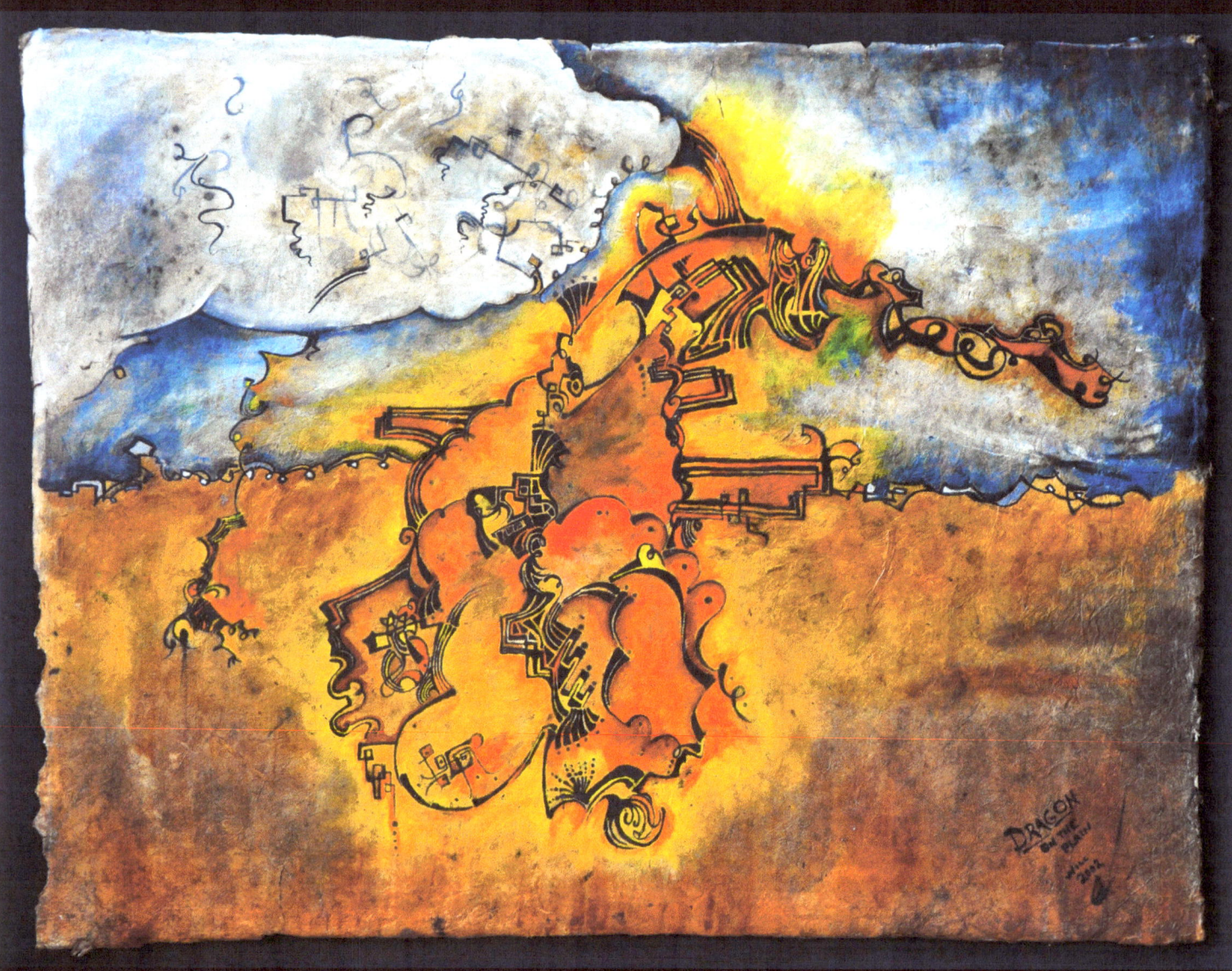

DRAGON ON THE PLAIN 26X19.5" (66X50 CM), OIL ON PAPER, 2002

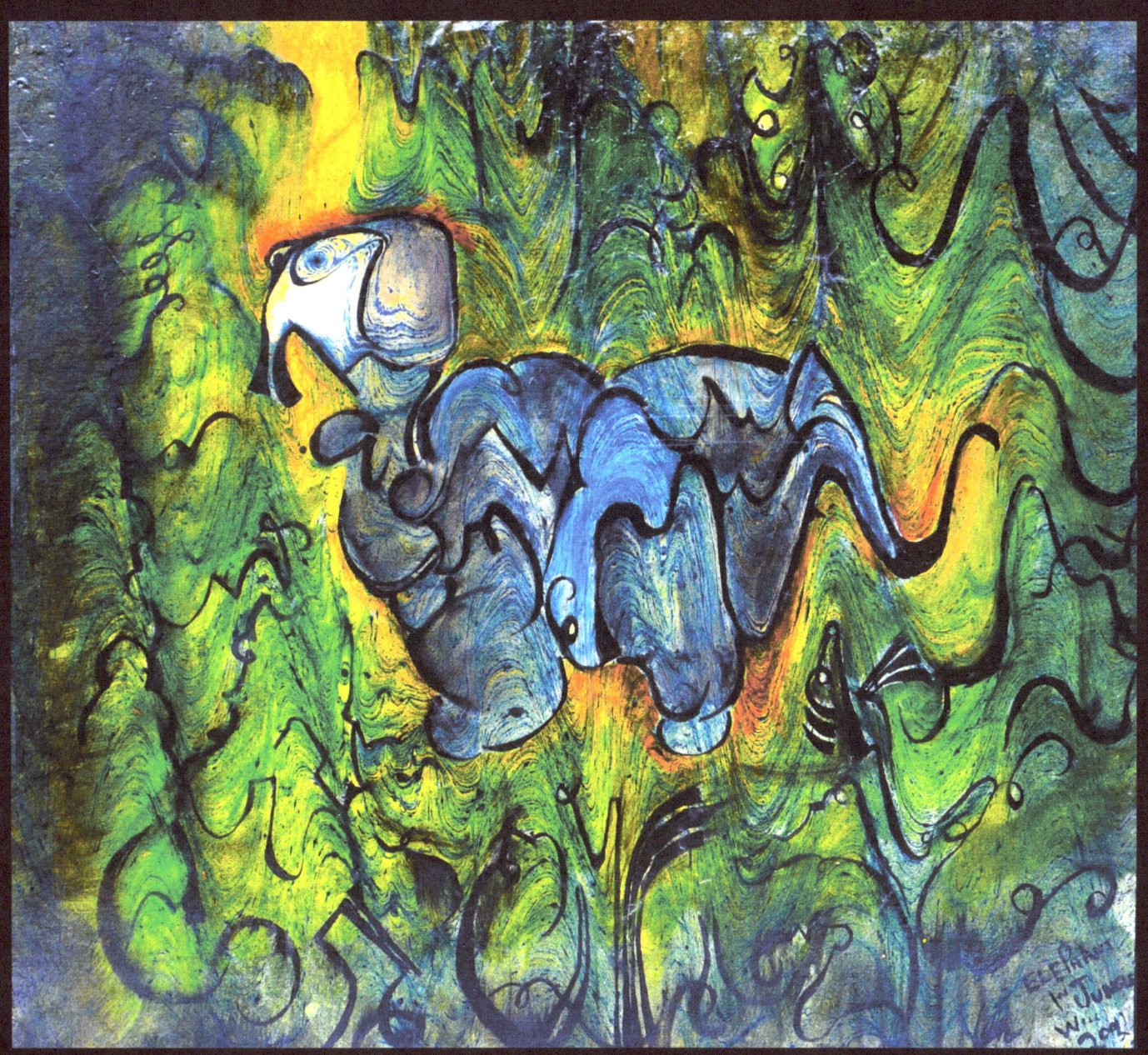

ELEPHANT IN THE JUNGLE SIZE LARGE (CM), OIL ON PAPER, 2002

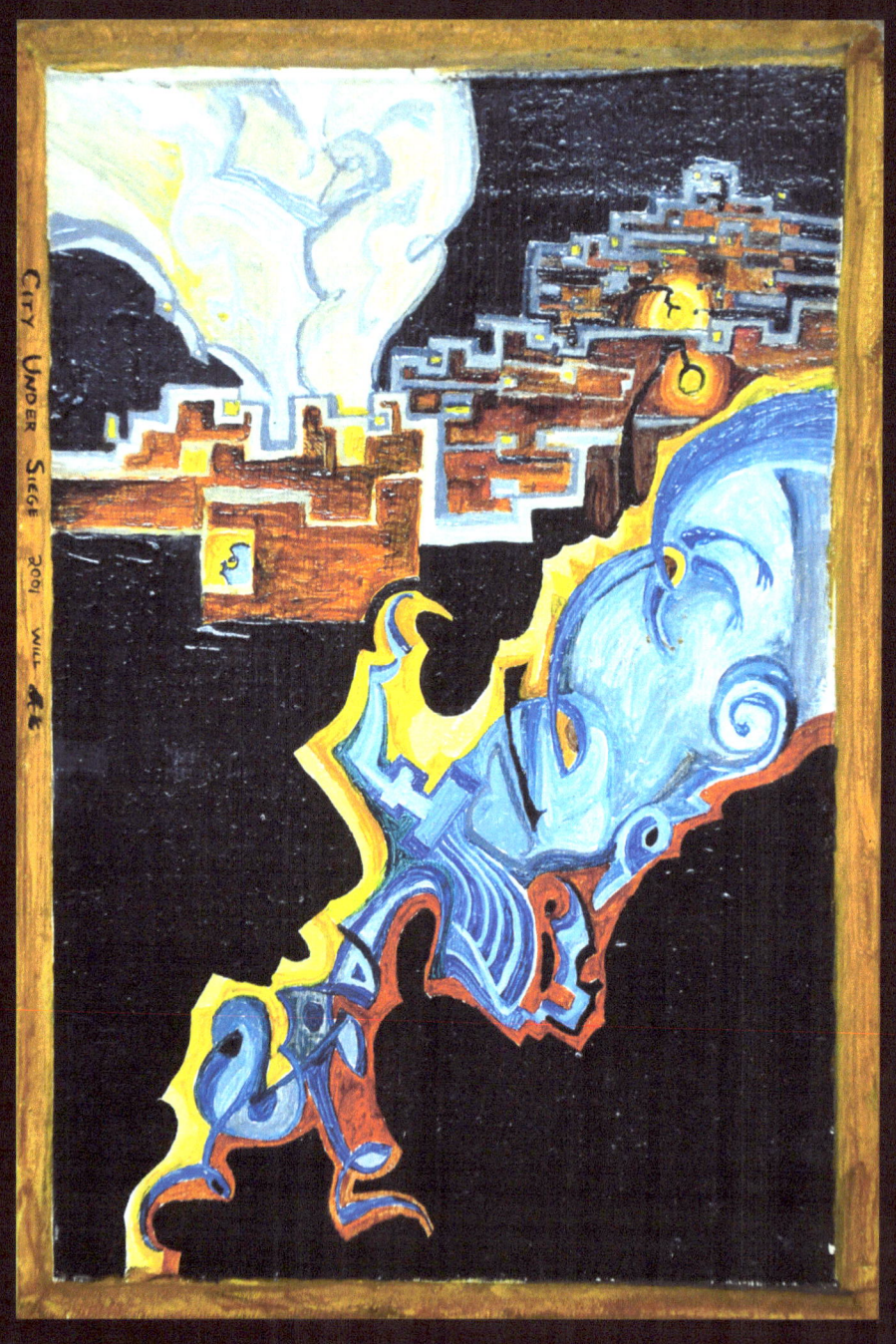

CITY UNDER SIEGE 6.5X9.5" (17X24 CM), OIL ON WOOD, 2001

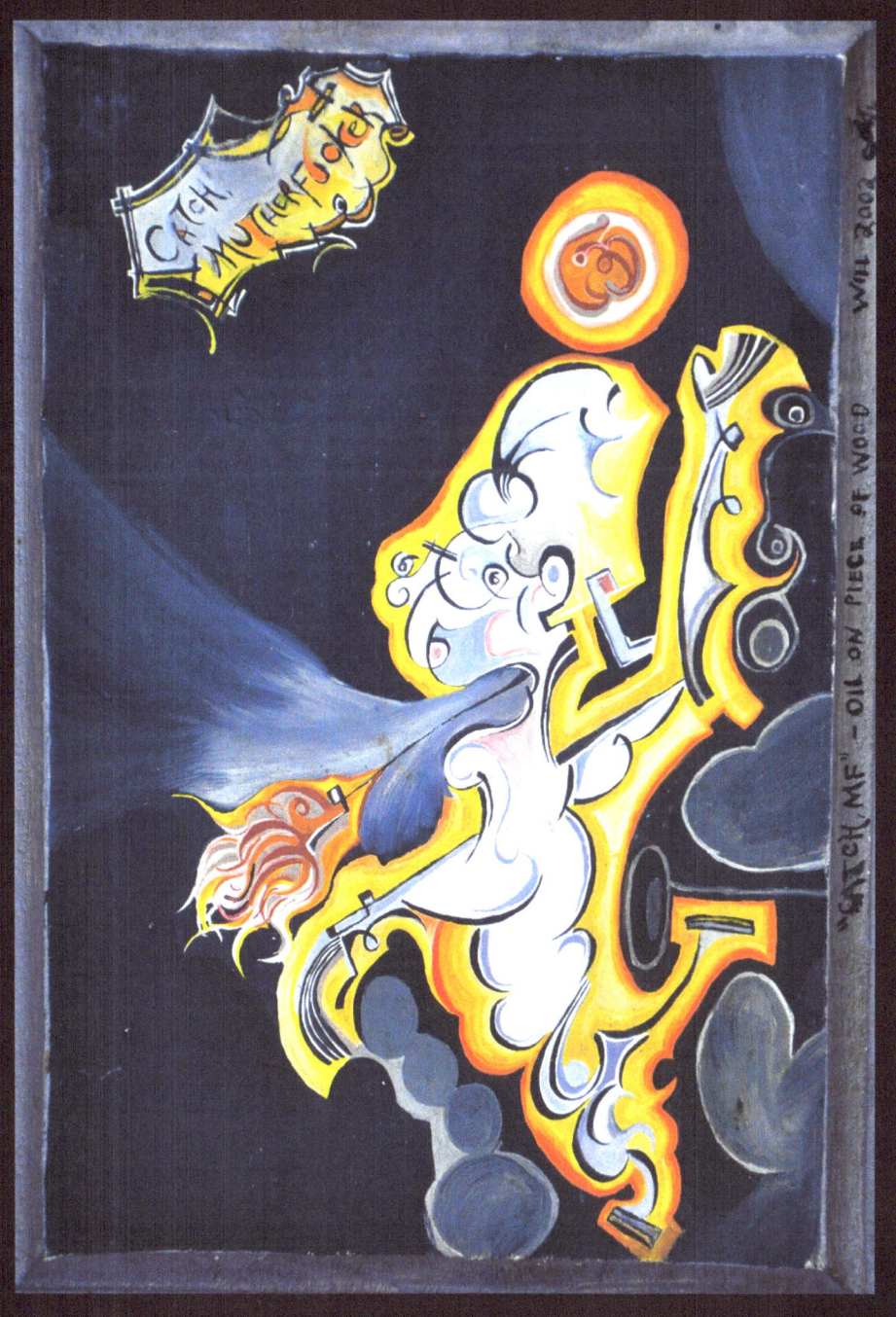

CATCH, MUTHERFUCKER 6.5X9.5" (17X24 CM), OIL ON WOOD, 2002

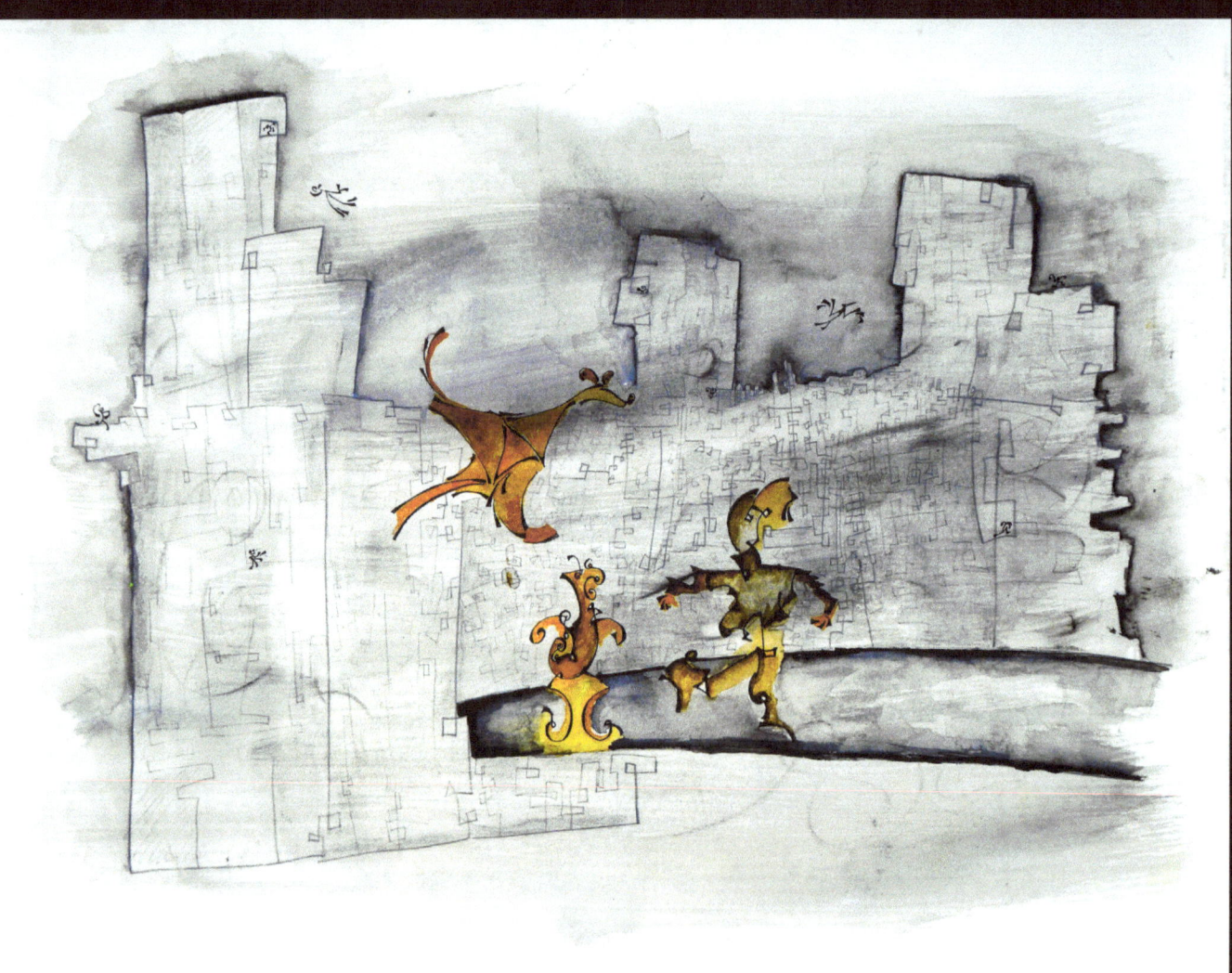

THREE FIGURES IN THE CITY 16X12" (30X41 CM), PENCIL, INK AND WATERCOLOR ON PAPER, 2003

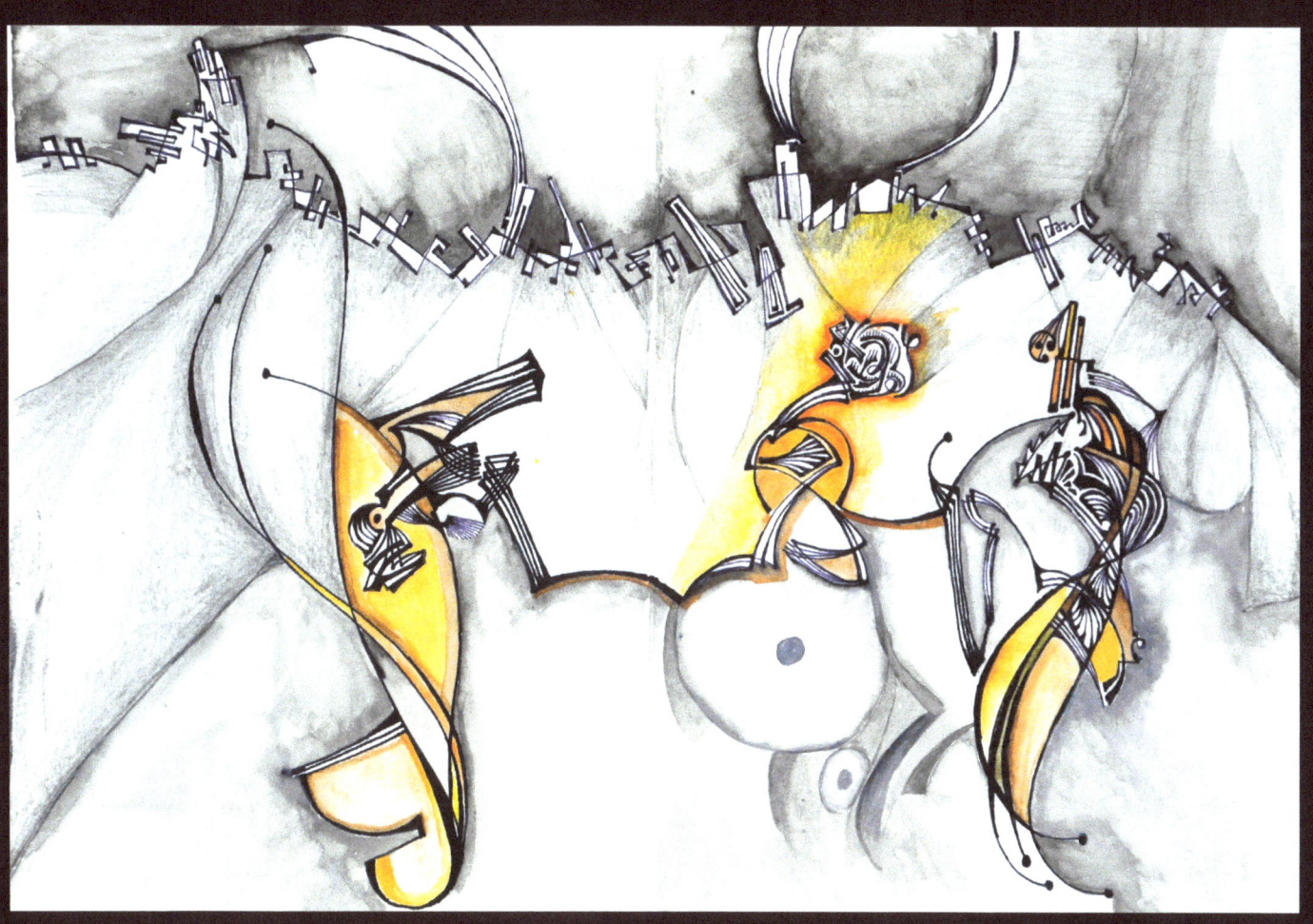

THREE MORE FIGURES IN THE CITY 15X10" (38X24 CM), PENCIL, INK AND WATERCOLOR ON PAPER, 2004

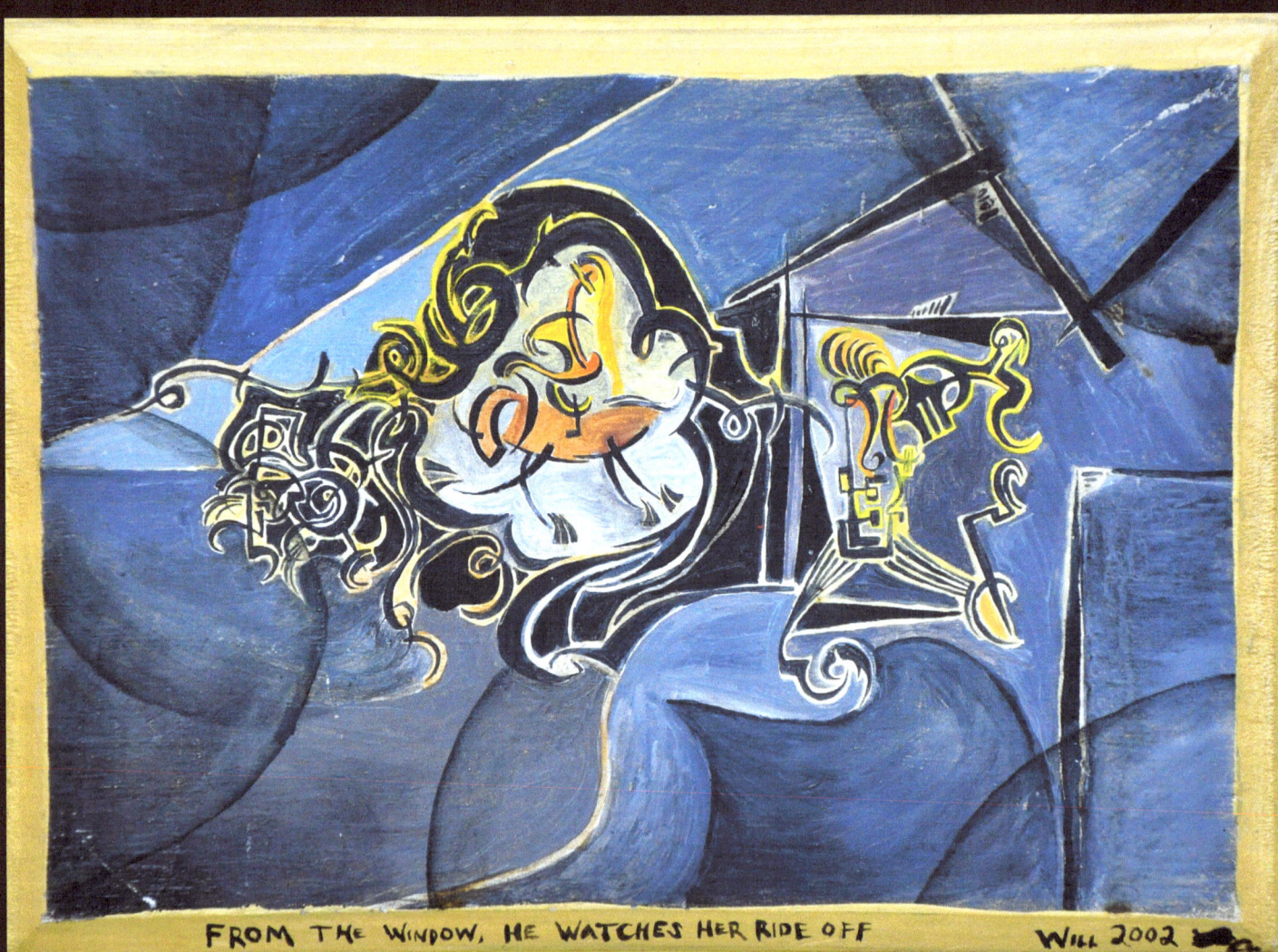

FROM THE WINDOW, HE WATCHES HER RIDE OFF   WILL 2002

FROM THE WINDOW, HE WATCHES HER RIDE OFF 9.5X6.5" (24X17 CM), OIL ON WOOD, 2001

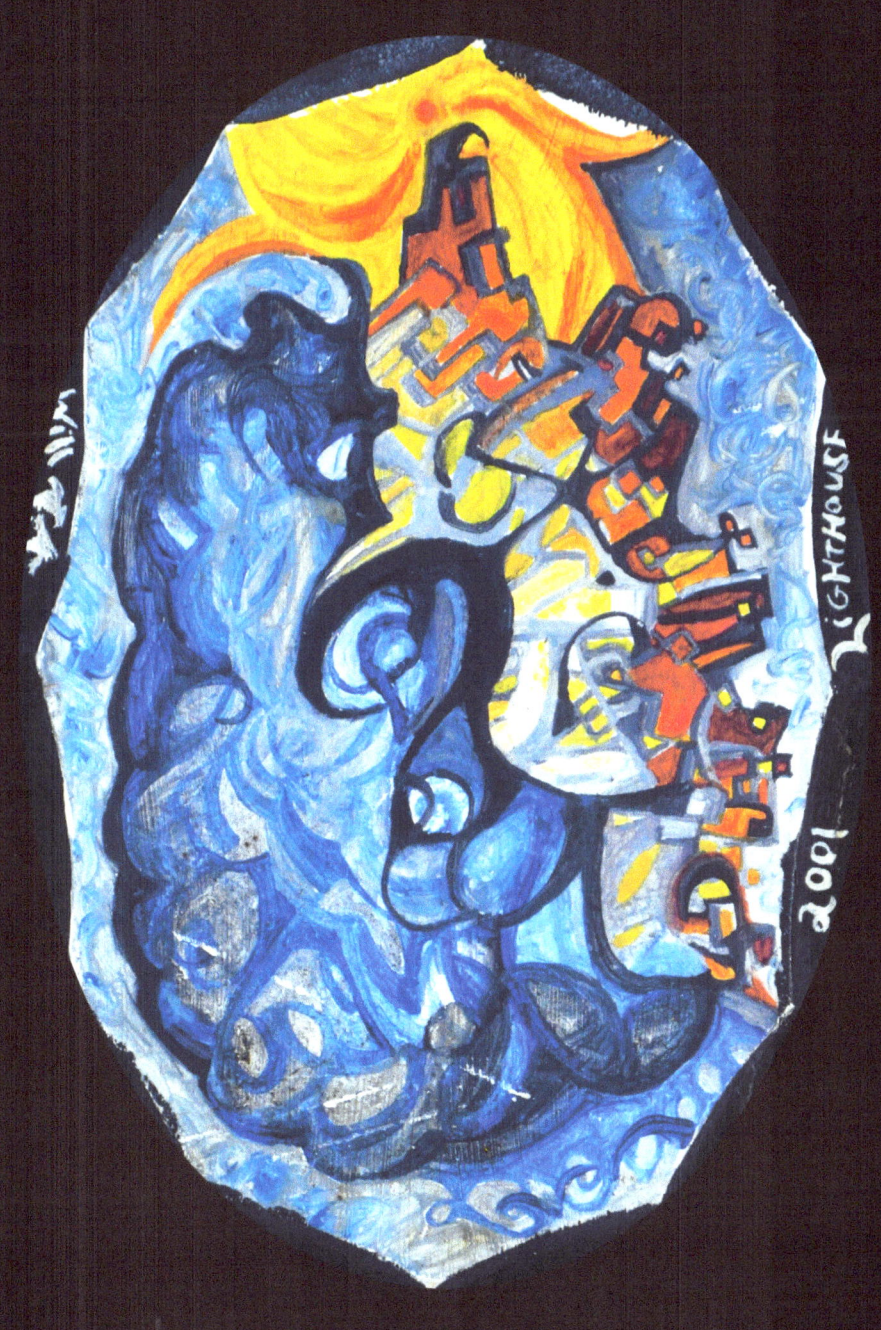

LIGHTHOUSE 7.5X9.5" (17X24 CM), OIL ON WOOD, 2001

MICROWAVES

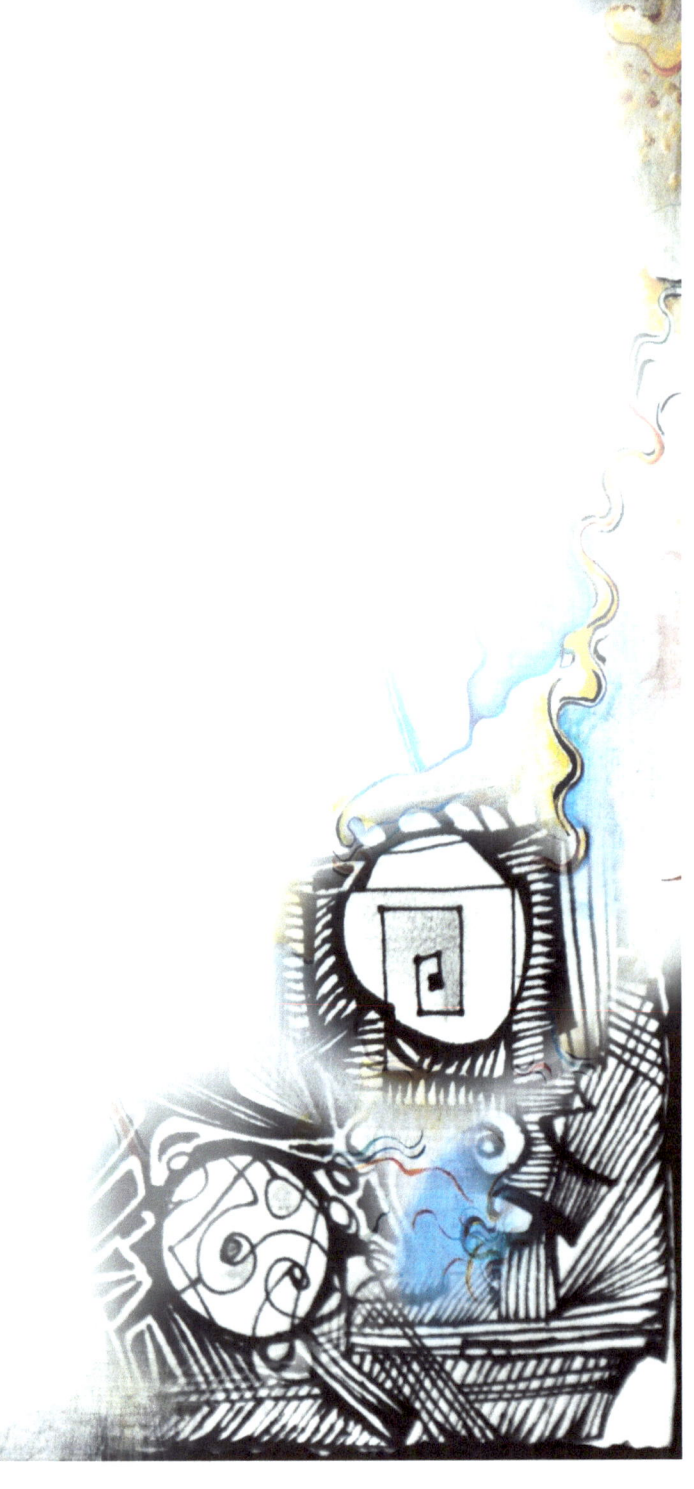

In the beginning was Chaos
I told you, you can't know
In ancient Hesiod
As you love men
From Chaos came Eros, then Gaia.
As men do not make love
Eros, desire, existed
As men are flat like paper
When there were no stars,
And you did not take offense
A moment without earth,
Because I dropped a plate
Eros floated through the universe,
And answered me with a kiss
Without male or female,
The goddess smiled, hating words
Without gods,
And I stopped ranting.
And without substance,
If I am going to be foolish
Coming into us from the void.
In my own kitchen
In 1965 Arno Penzias and Robert Wilson
And if you have made your point
Detected Hesiod's residue of appetite
Aren't you done?
Called it microwave background noise.

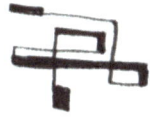

REASONING

I could refute you
To make you wrong seem
Somehow, by talking,
But that's unlikely.

You're still mistaken.
One kiss to correct you
A kiss I expect to
Piss you off
But still you like me.

I will settle this issue
When I kiss you,
You mere man,
A sorry condition.

Willing chump,
I advised you
In advance of no romance
And bad intentions.

I said I would kiss, not speak,
But I spoke, not kissed:
But my point, you get it.

This moment is magnetic.
You, stuck here waiting.
How pathetic.

You must believe me.
Otherwise, you'd leave, see?

I make my point
When I disappoint
Your anticipation.

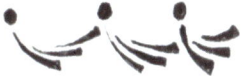

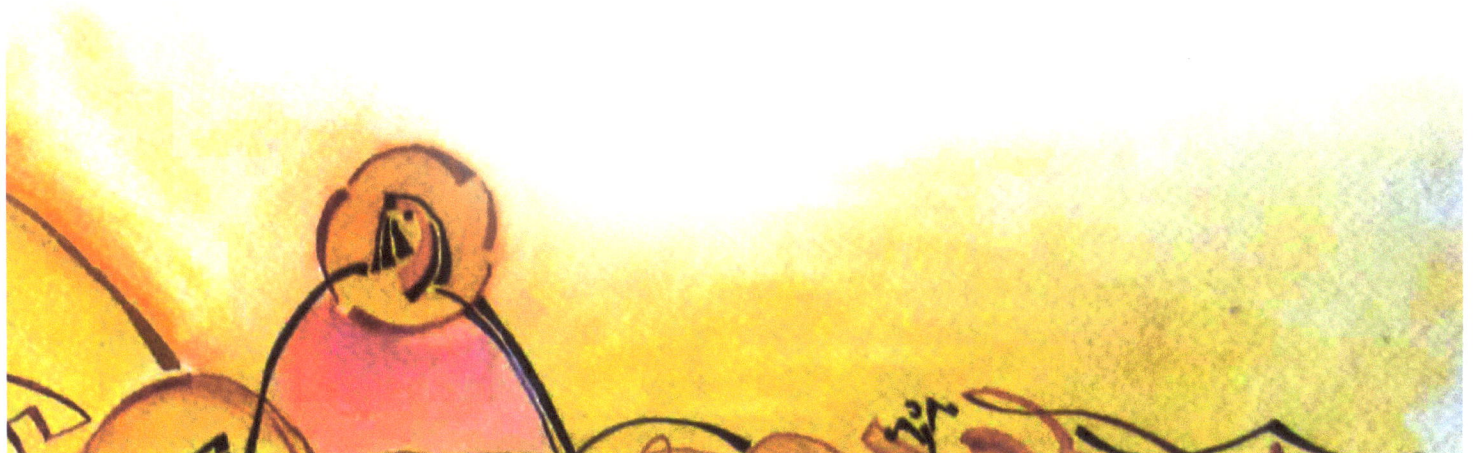

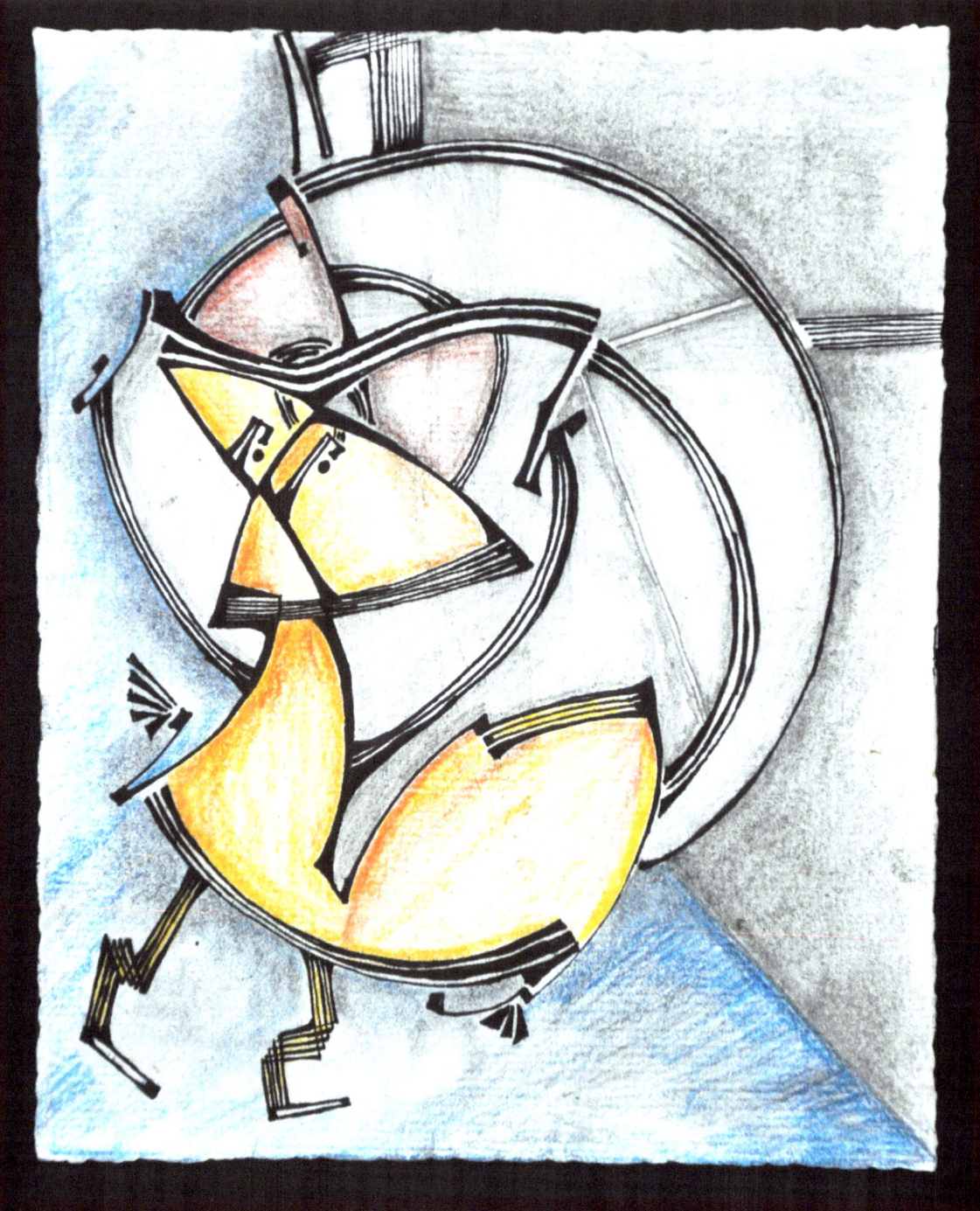

CIRCLE OF THE SIMPLE 7.5X9.5" (19X24 CM), PENCIL AND INK ON PAPER, 2004

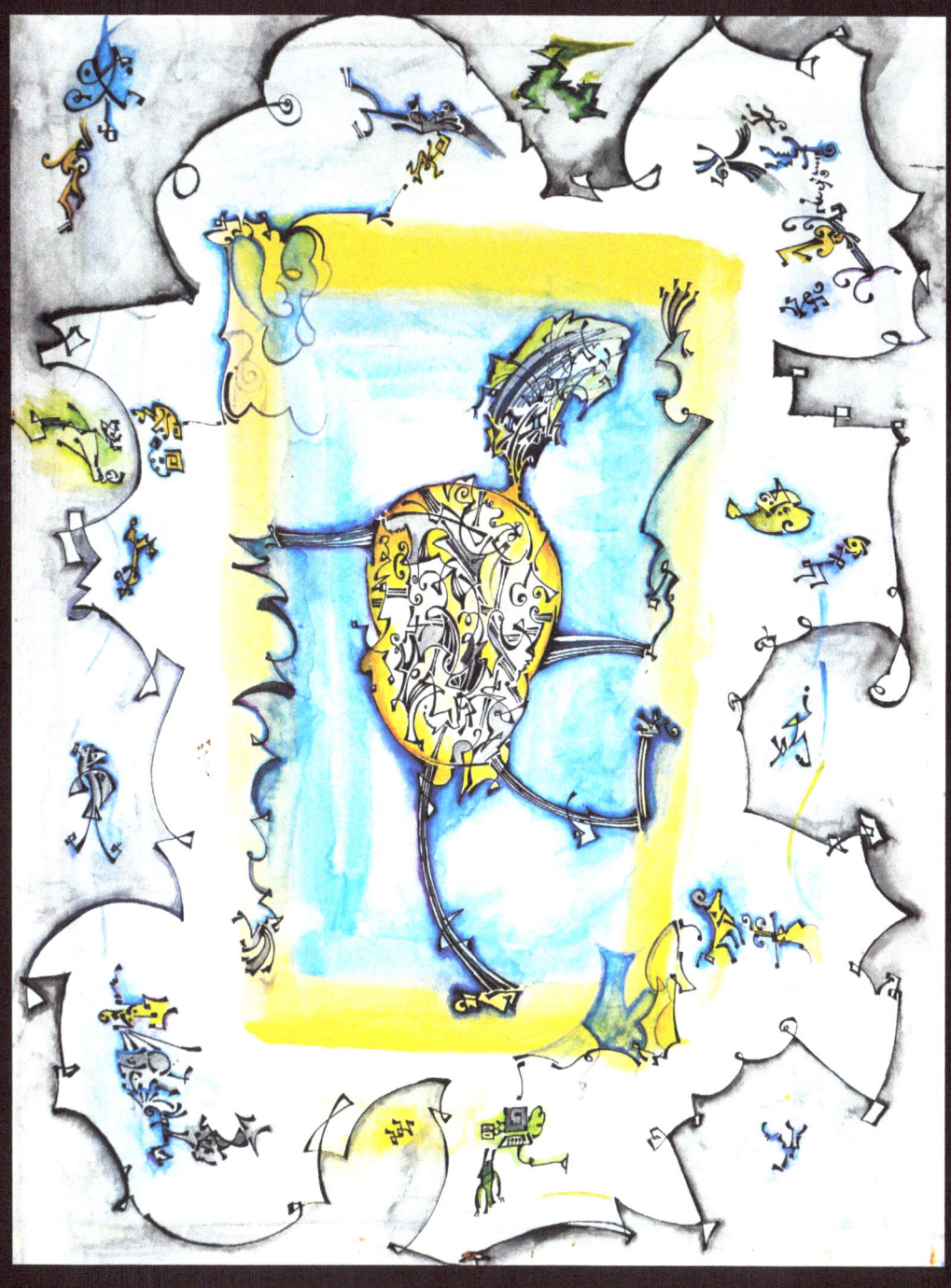

THROUGH THE DOOR 12X16" (30X41 CM), WATERCOLOR ON PAPER, 1999

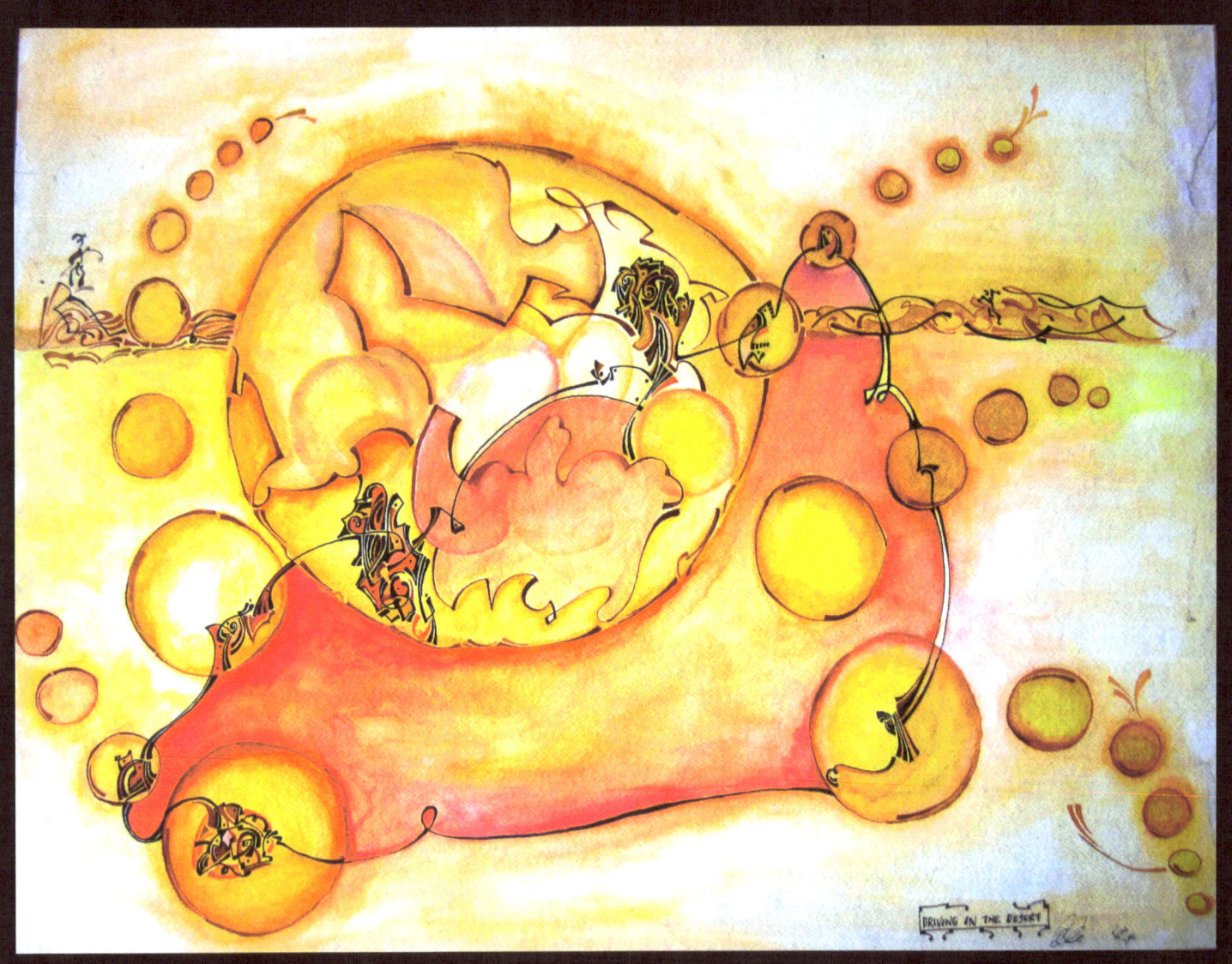

DRIVING IN THE DESERT 24X18" (61X46 CM), WATERCOLOR ON PAPER, 2002

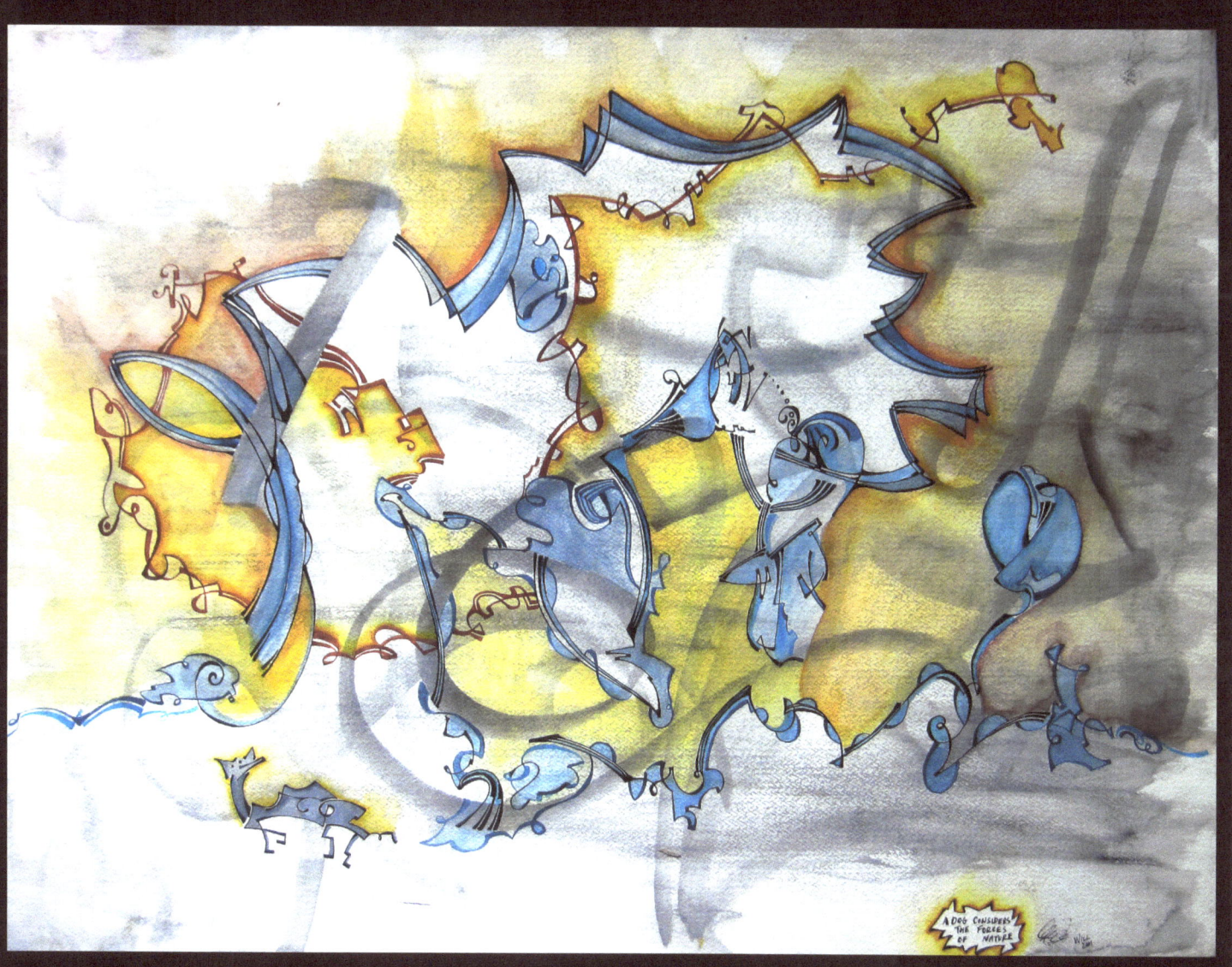

A DOG CONSIDERS THE FORCES OF NATURE 24X18" (61X46 CM), WATERCOLOR ON PAPER, 2002

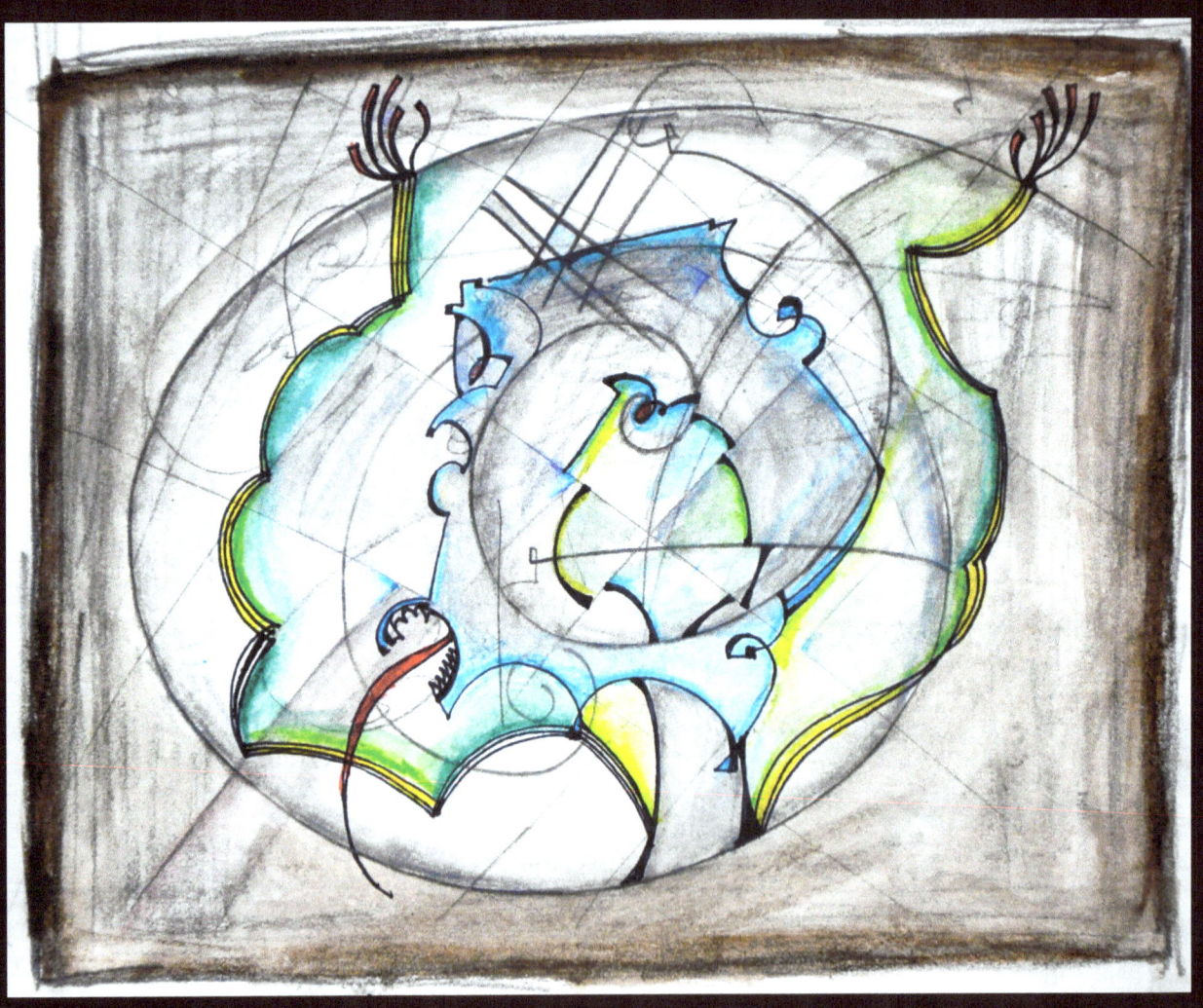

HANDS UP, TONGUE OUT 10X8" (25X20 CM), INK, PENCIL AND WATERCOLOR ON PAPER, 2012

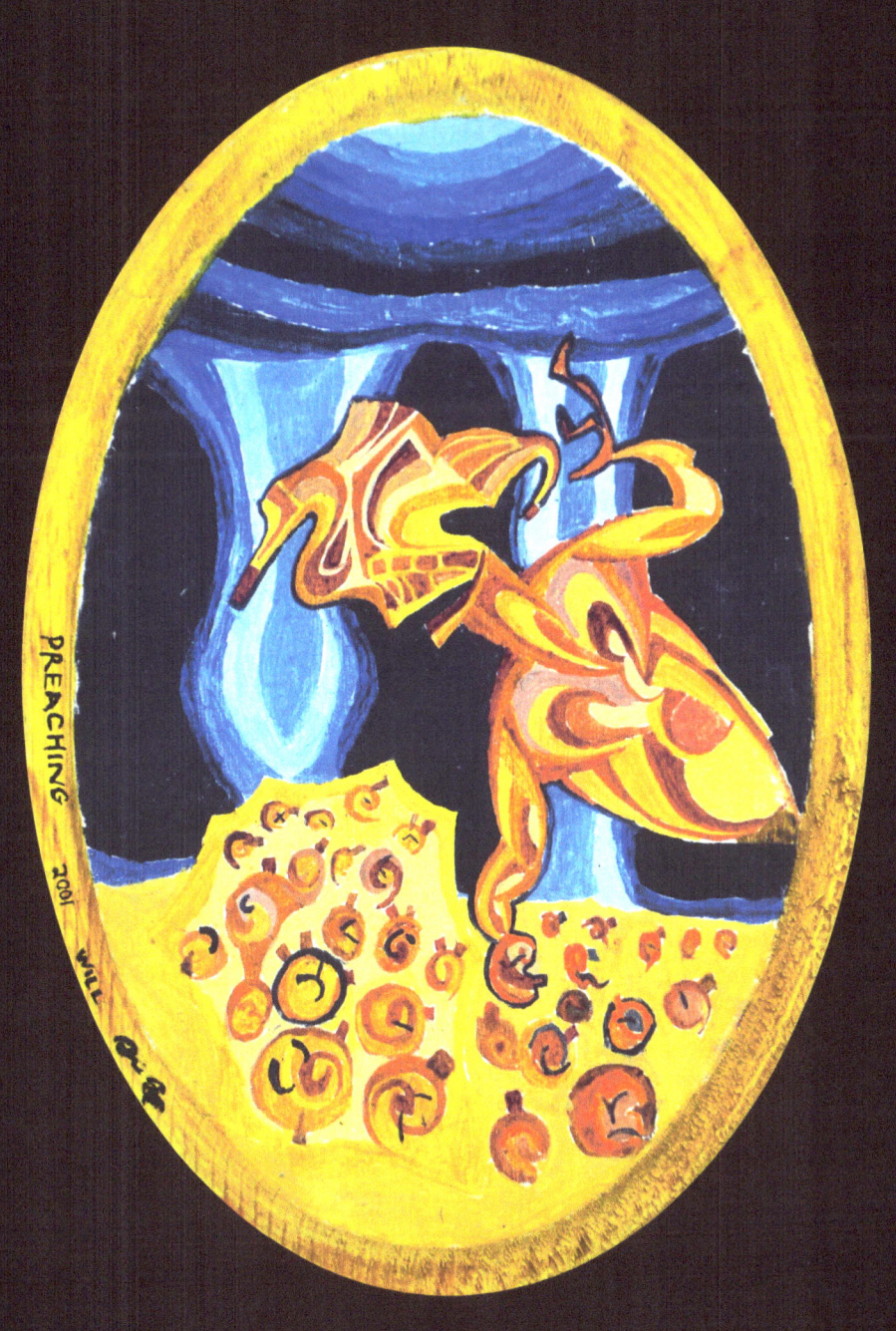

PREACHING 4.5X6.5" (11X16 CM), OIL ON WOOD, 2001

FURTHER THAN THAT

The moment the robe
Fell to the floor
Laid an egg.

The egg of incident
Was buried by urges
That live in the moment.

The urges diverged:
Lust going left,
Not going right.

In the opening between
The memory hatched,
Drinking new light.

The worm feasted
On my leafy eyes
Until well after noon.

In the frank essence of me
Seen only in dark
The worm made a cocoon.

A moment buried,
Re-born as memory,
Transformed into dream.

Moment to memory,
Memory to fantasy,
Fantasy to story,
Where the scent went.
She flew away long ago.

Lighter in the fog of her
I can drift up or down.
It depends on your hand,
As on my robe,
Falling off,
Away from a shoulder
That could have been yours.

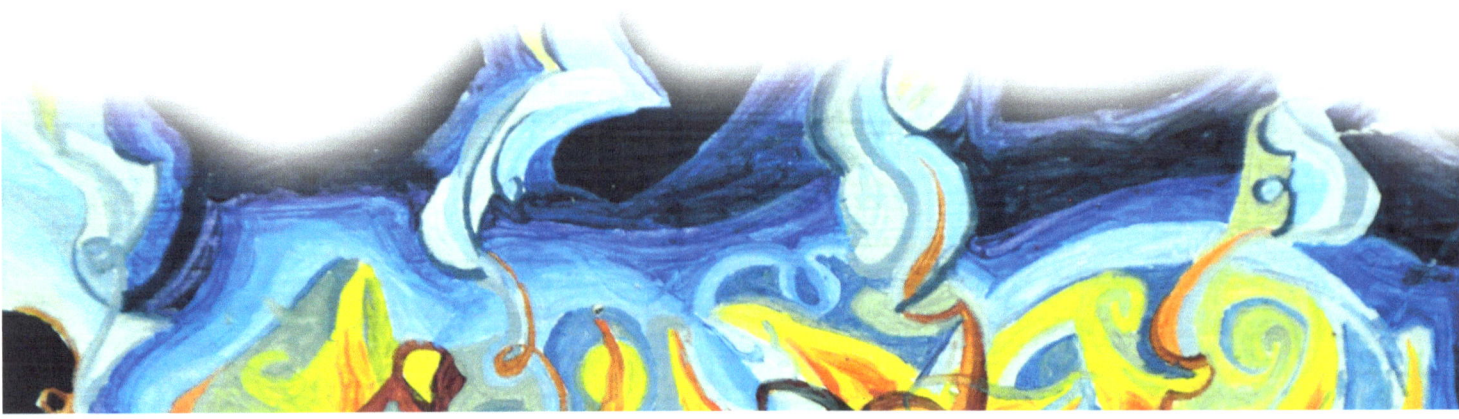

PERFECT AT LEAST

"Is this your highbrow alternative
to Classmates? The past has been
navigated already."

Like a beast,
I thought, what?
With grain in a bowl
Filling the gut,
Late in the Fall,
The season to rut?

The now and the soon
But never the then,
That's a barn.
If you don't bleed
You know no harm.

A perfect day
Not a video
You can rewind
And review and play back
Too twisted in mind
Too rooted in thought
Never so clear,
Never so flat.

Blaspheme the past
While holding a grudge
Like a rope,
After you fell down a well.

That you I knew would
Say the you now is lost
And has slipped
And the beautiful you would
Hear me out
And savor and consider
And not be bitter
And would not be where you fell.

What beasts don't know
And gods don't need
Is that what I sent.

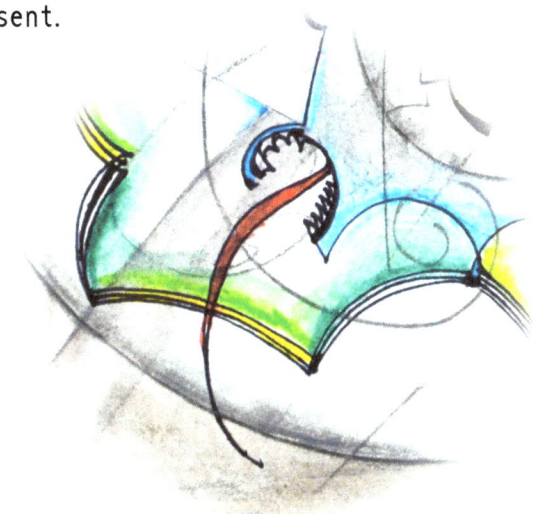

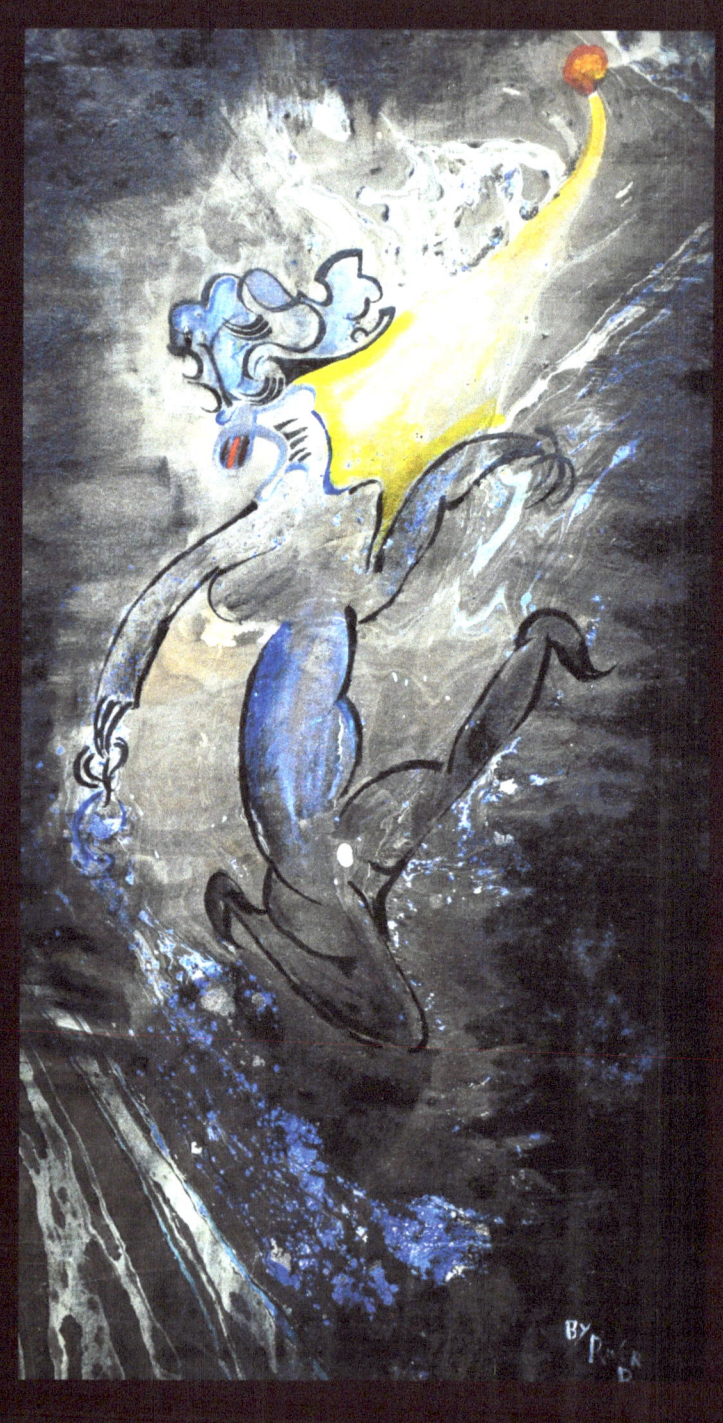

MOONLIGHT SHOWER 9X19.5" (23X50 CM), OIL ON PAPER, 2003

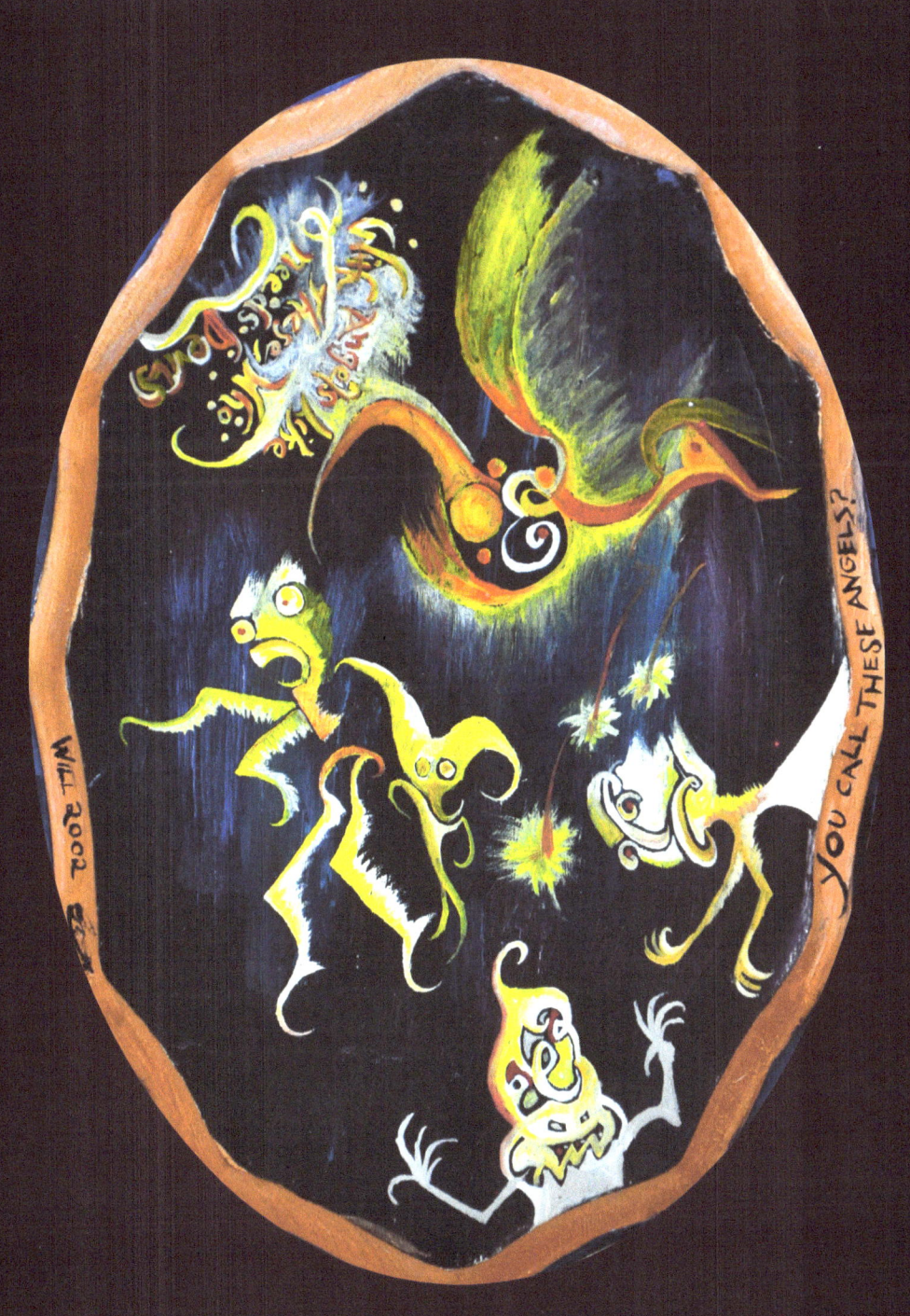

YOU CALL THESE ANGELS? 6.5x9.5" (17x24 CM), OIL ON WOOD, 2001

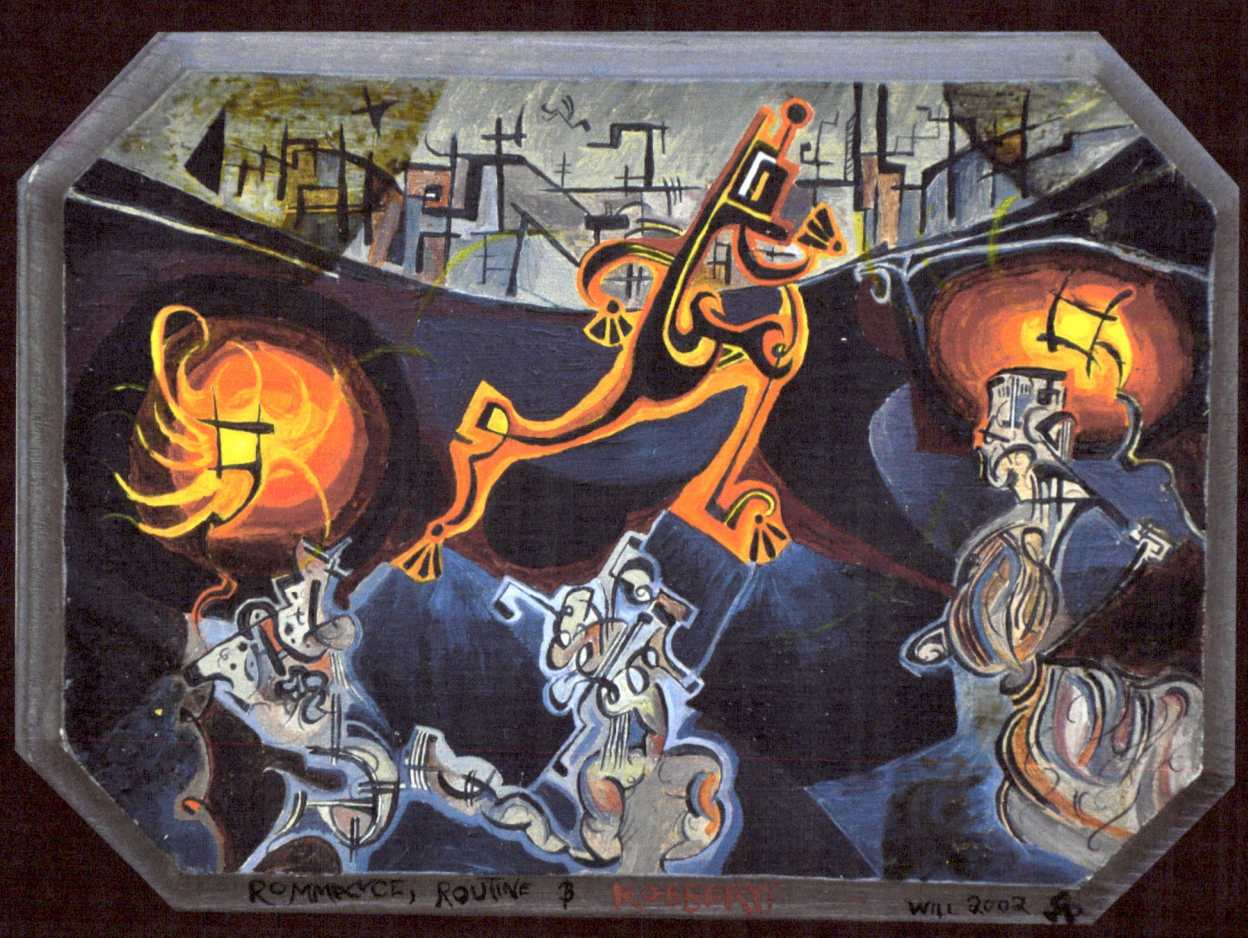

ROMMANCE, ROUTINE, ROBBERY 9.5X6.5" (24X17 CM), OIL ON WOOD, 2002

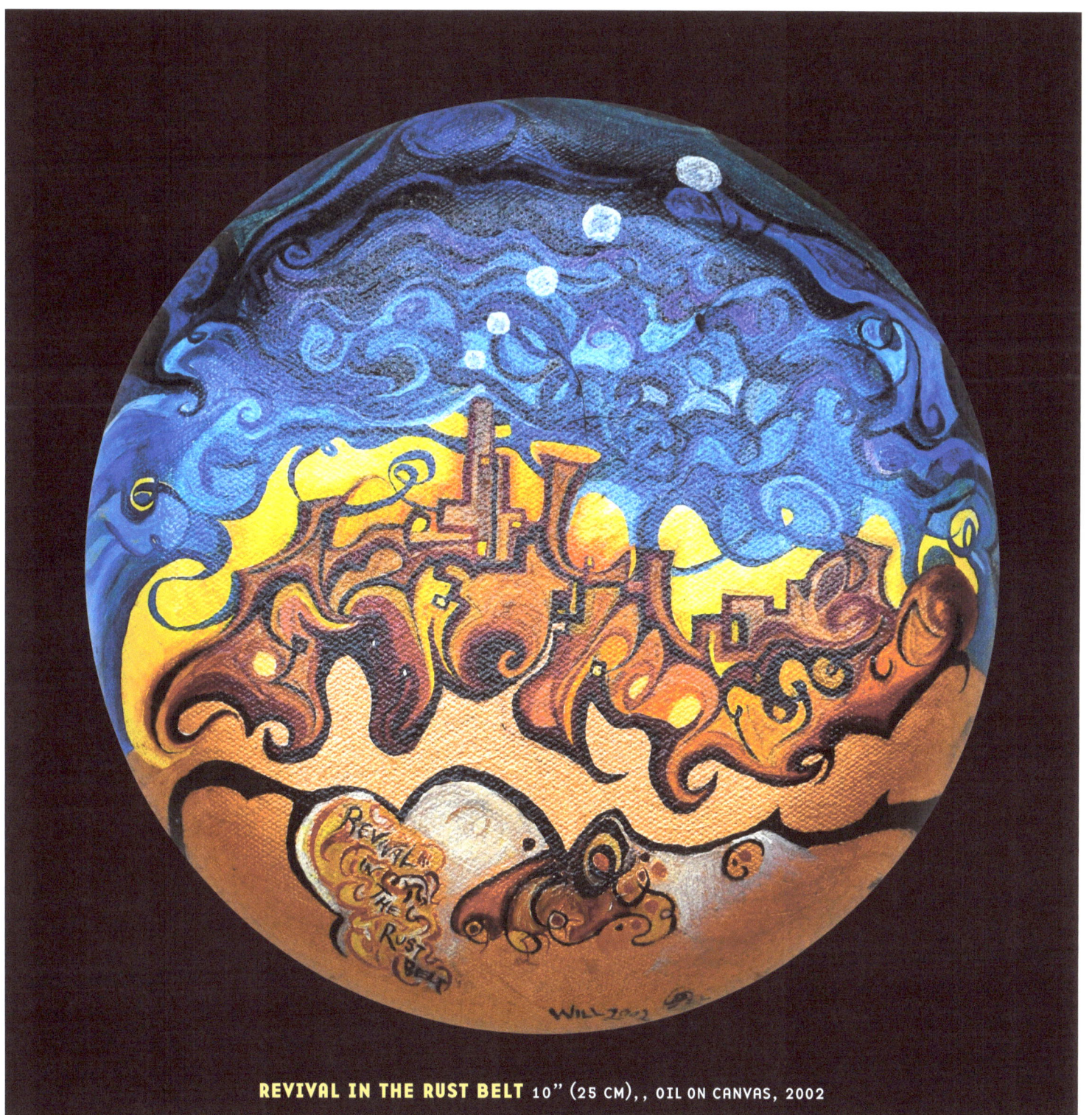

REVIVAL IN THE RUST BELT 10" (25 CM),, OIL ON CANVAS, 2002

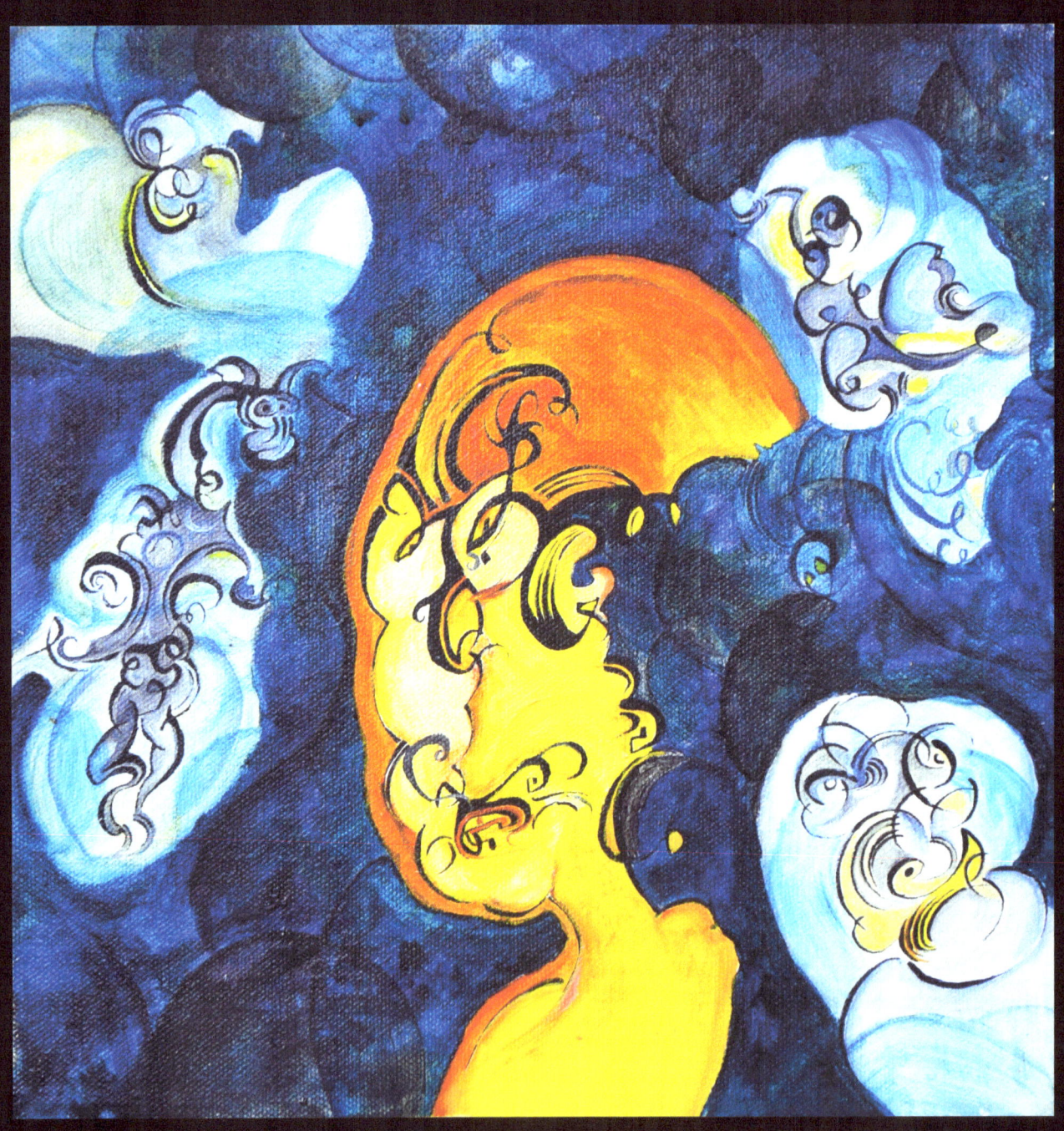

IN THE COURT OF THE SAVAGE KING 12x12" (31x31 CM), OIL ON CANVAS, 2003

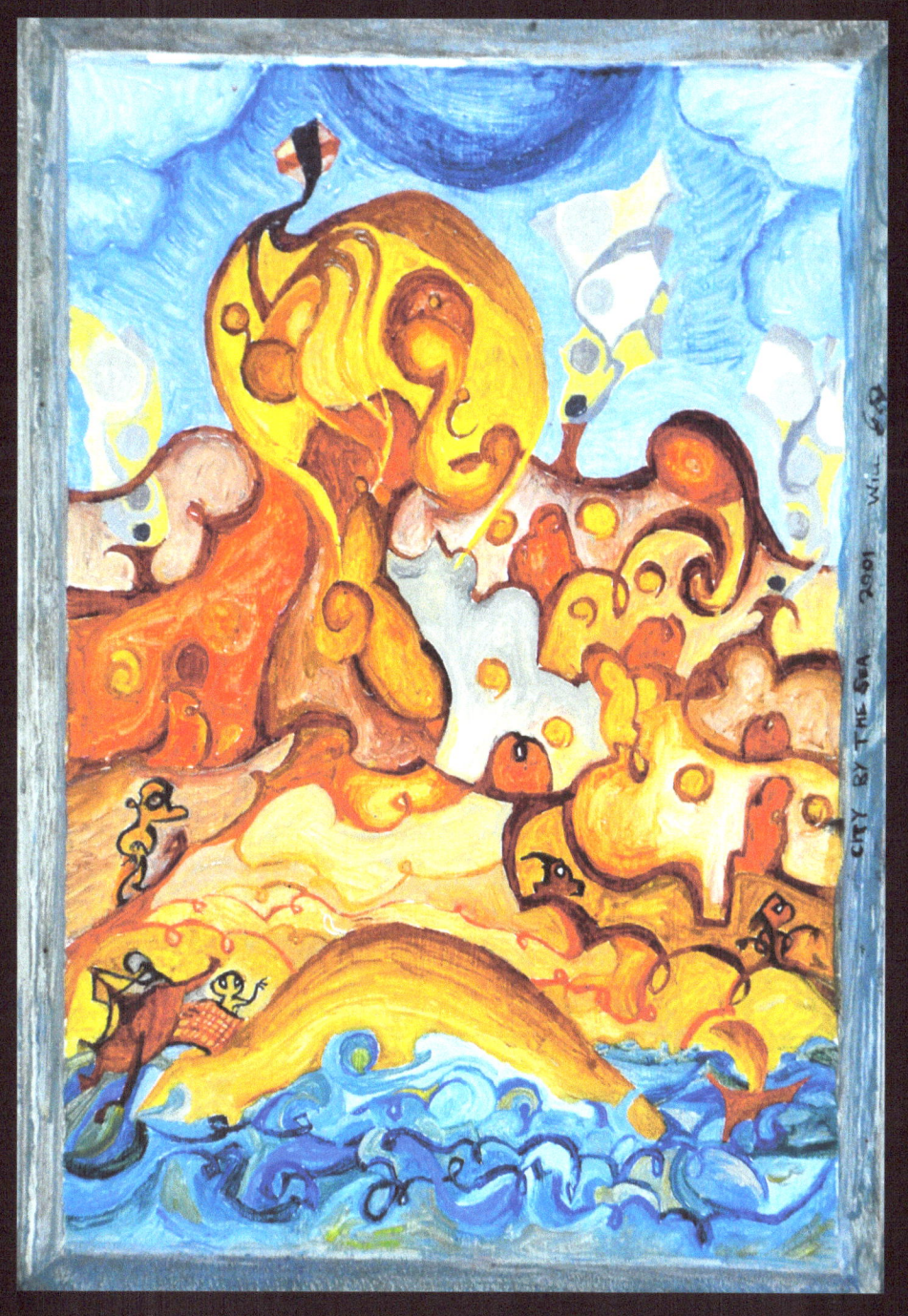

CITY BY THE SEA 6.5X9.5" (17X24 CM), OIL ON WOOD, 2001

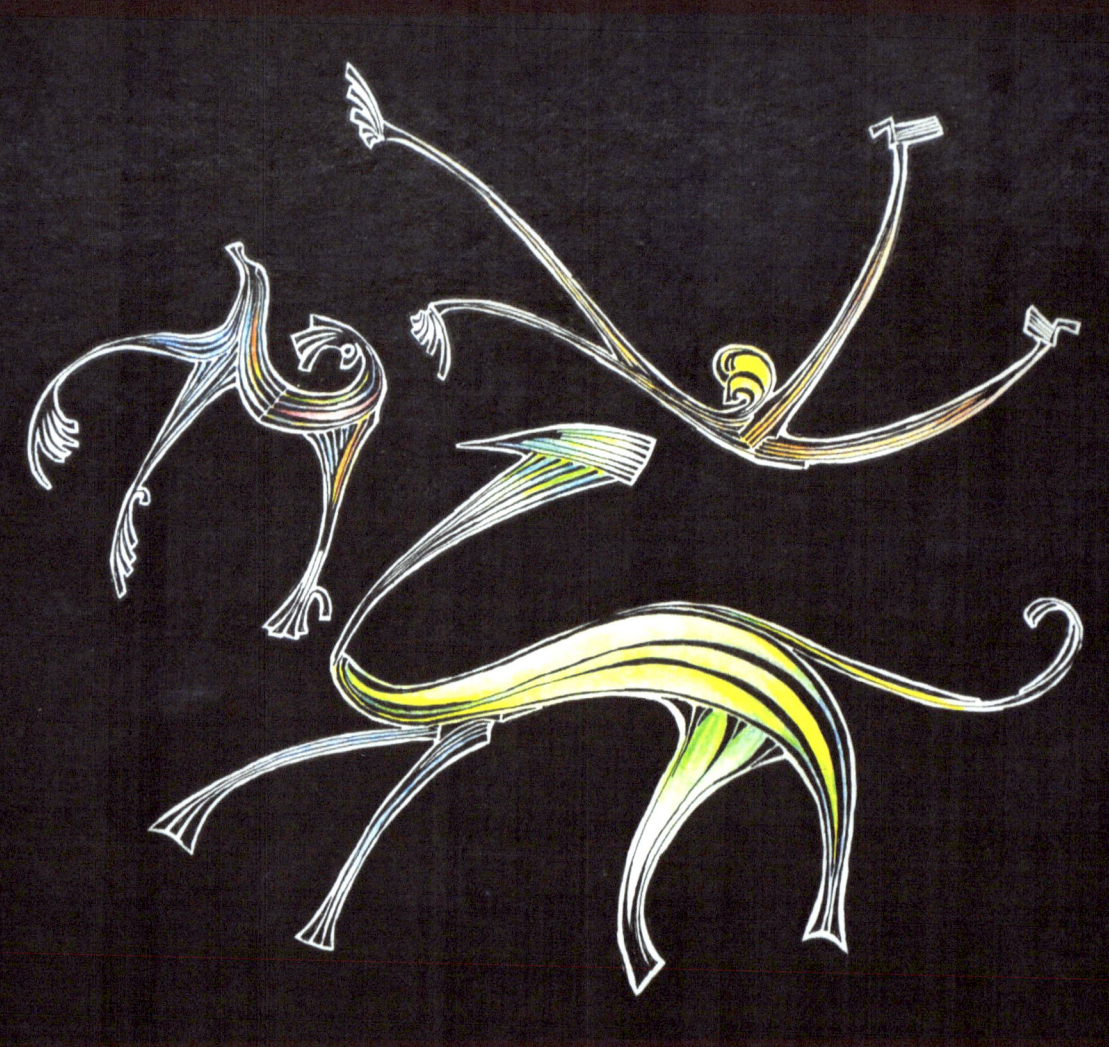

THREE CRITTERS 12X9" (23X30 CM), INK AND PENCIL ON PAPER, 1997

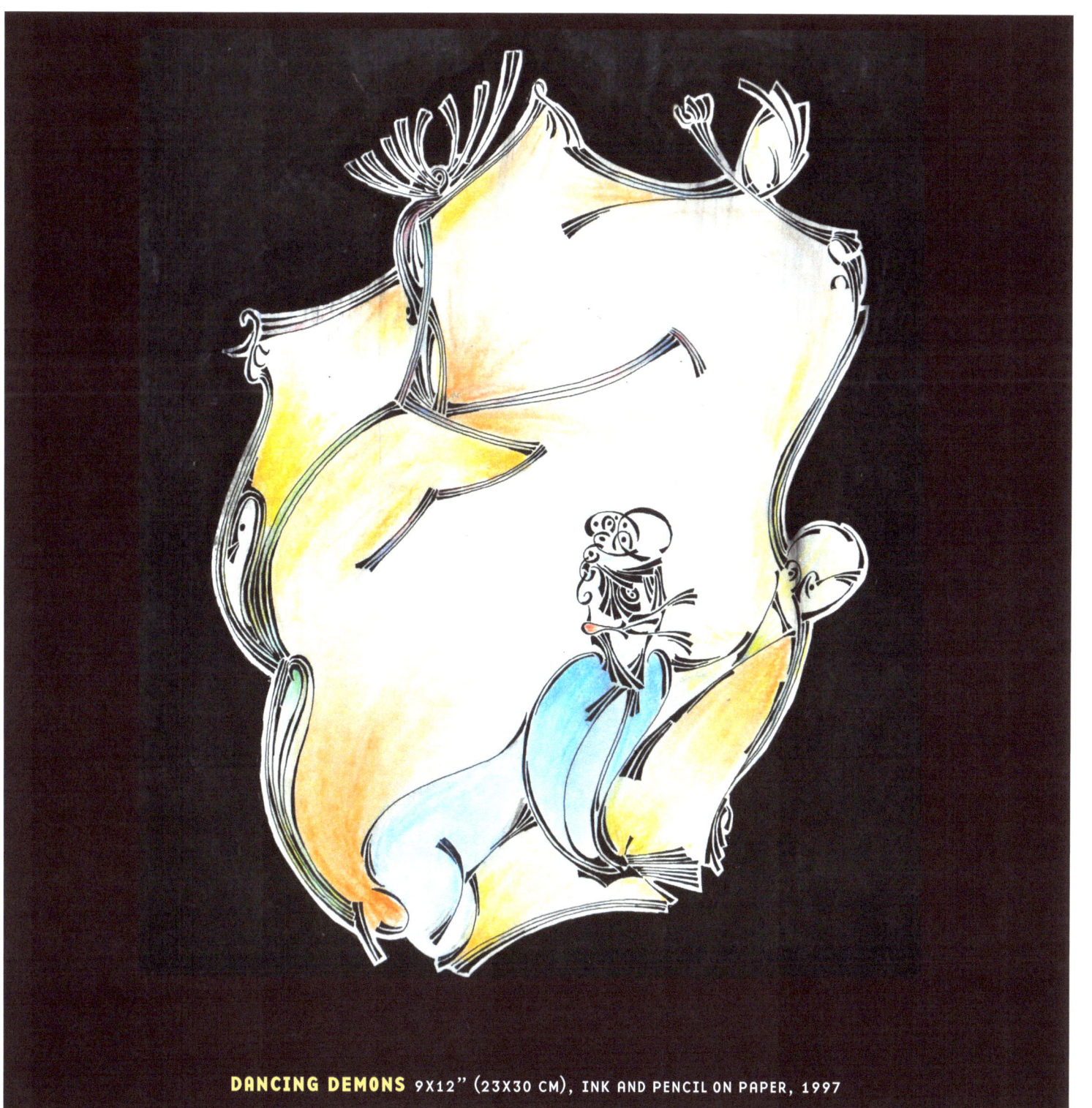

DANCING DEMONS 9X12" (23X30 CM), INK AND PENCIL ON PAPER, 1997

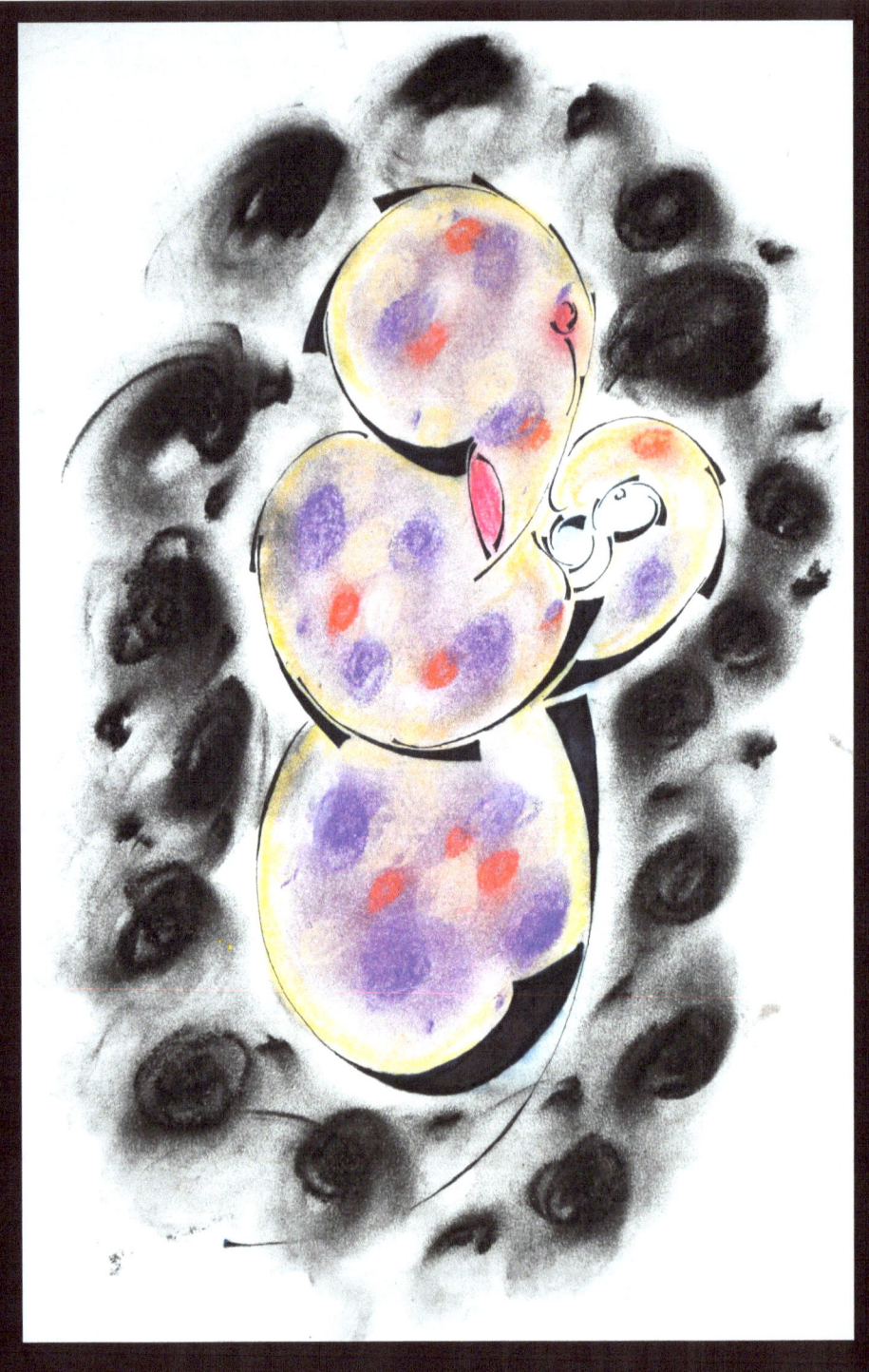

MOTHER AND BABY 12X16" (30X41 CM), CHARCOL ON PAPER, 1995

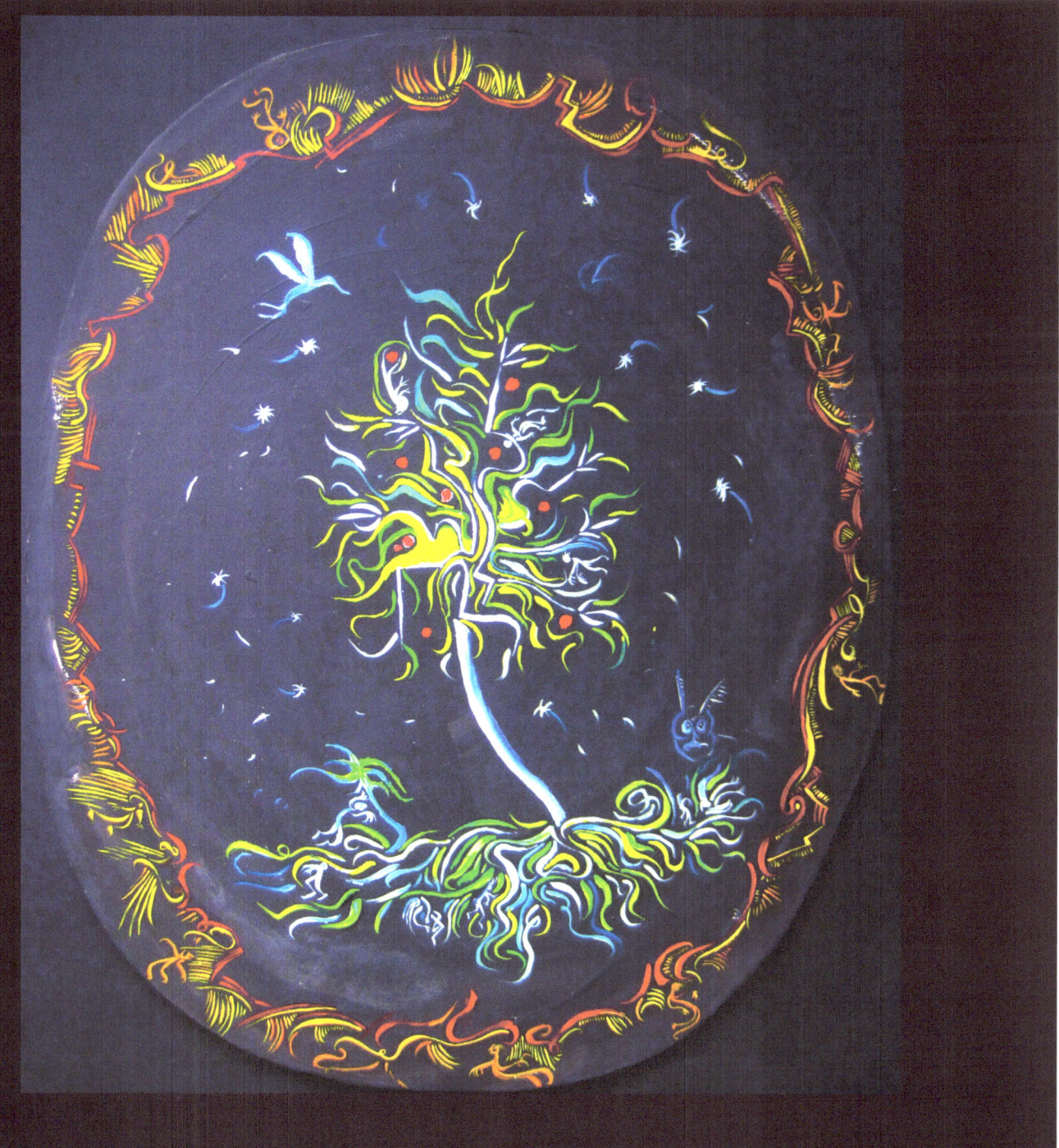

MANY HIDDEN CRITTERS, A BIRD AND A TROLL 17X20" (43X50 CM), OIL ON WOOD, 2012

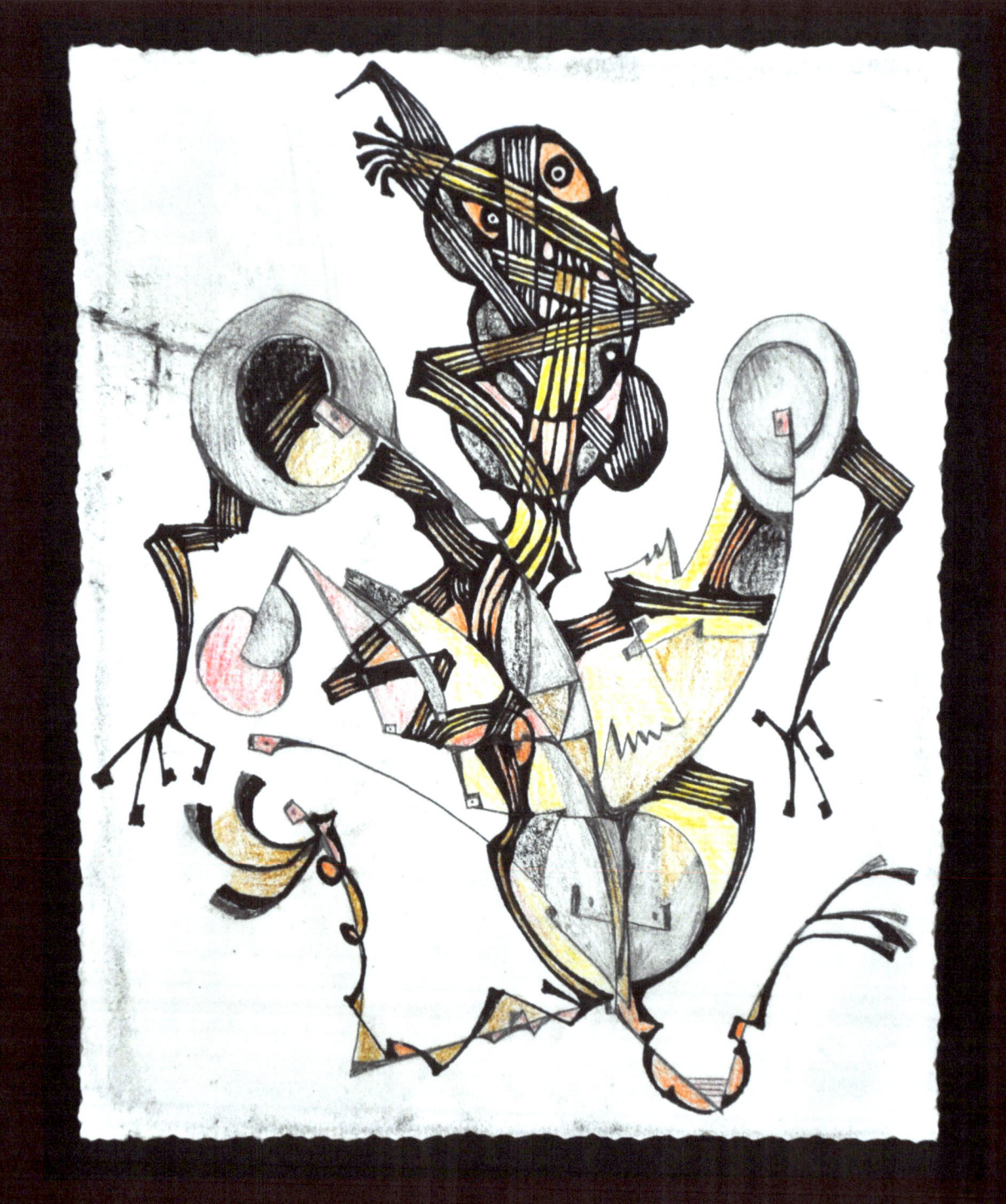

ELEGANT CLUTZ 7.5X8.5" (19X22 CM), INK AND PENCIL ON PAPER, 2004

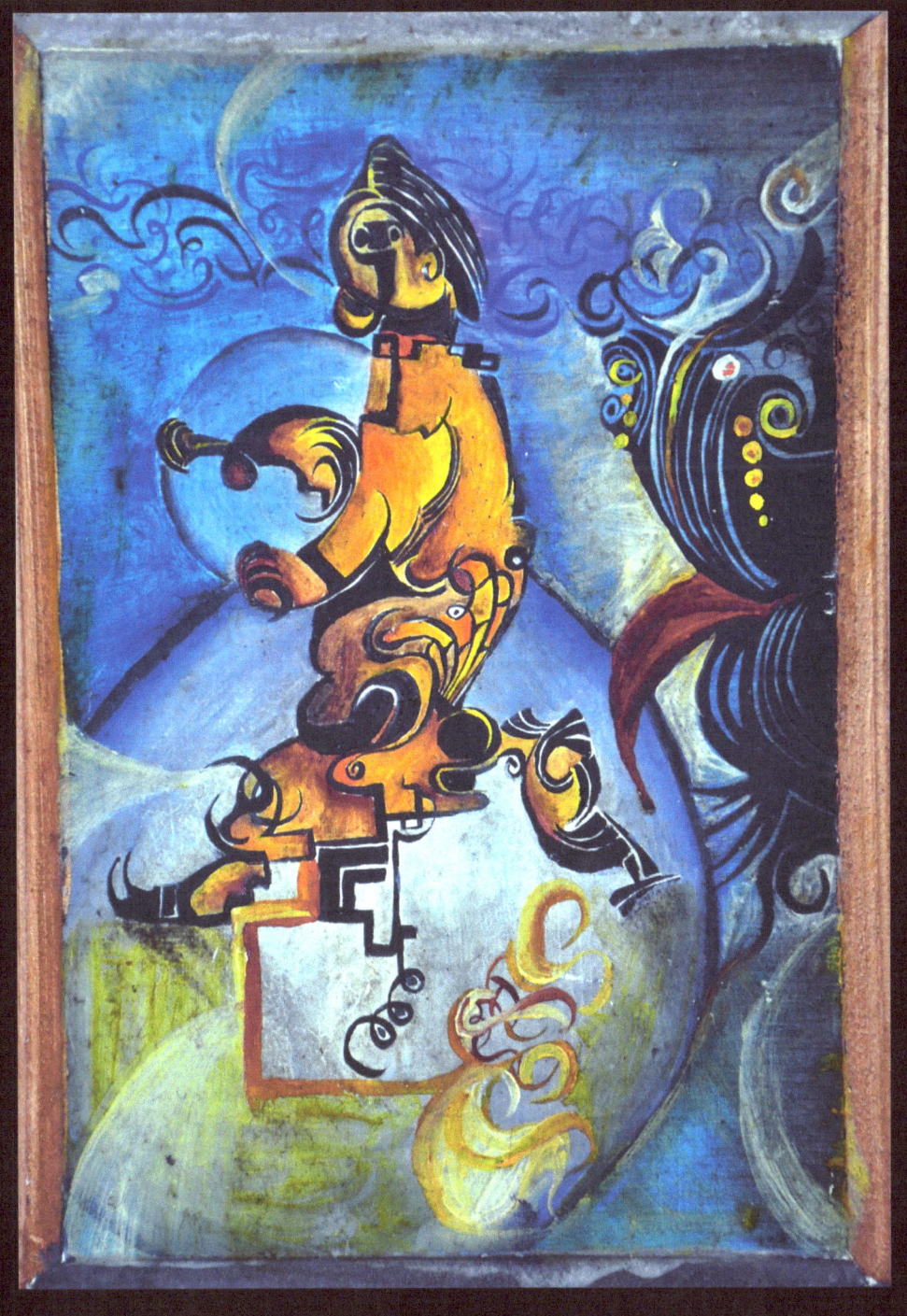

LICKED BY A SHADOW PUPPET 6.5X9.5" (17X24 CM), OIL ON WOOD, 2002

IMPRINT

When the egg breaks
And the gosling emerges
Ready for imprint,
The first connection.

The adolescent encounters
Instinct only in urges
That can be turned in one
Of a thousand directions.

By the neighbor's pool
The day that I spent
I was allowed to stare
Feeling the intensity of her skin.

Or the day after school
Sexy as open-heart surgery
Two friends watching porn
I did not know existed until I walked in.

Scoffing on my memories this tame,
But stop. The principle also pertains
To your imprint, you as you broke shell
The crime they wouldn't let you tell,
For monsters, violence, on a child converged,
Amplified horror, when you emerged.

Home, examined, you as if on a slide,
"Like a bug," ten years later, you said.
He said, "Take a shower."
Monsters and fools should not define you.
You cannot let them have this power.
Ten years is long to be suppressed.
Ten years, when you did confide,
A strange way to fall in love,
There must be another reason
Why you are depressed.

You should get up and do something.
That much I knew. No one needed me before.
I could be with you, what else is there?
You said what you had to say.
Don't say it any more.

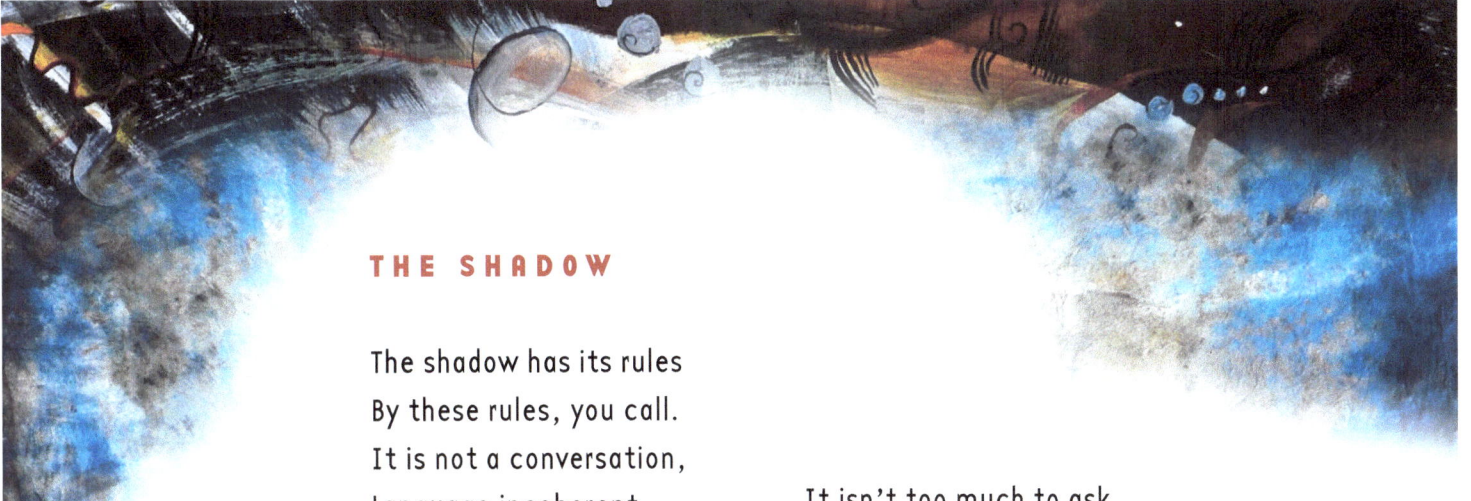

THE SHADOW

The shadow has its rules
By these rules, you call.
It is not a conversation,
Language incoherent,
Breathing in a phone
Until dawn, other than alone.

The shadow atrophies,
Recedes, months or years.
But when it reappears
With force of law,
By clear dictates
Will come another call.

These calls don't work
But they also don't fail
Any better or worse
Than yoga or drugs.
Some kind of mix you need
To survive your curse.

It isn't too much to ask.
You never call to chat.
You want ten hours a year from me.
When I did not call you back, murder.
Don't be kind in your goodbye.
Don't tell me not to blame myself.
You were murdered by me.
The killer gets no sympathy.

When you said, "It's not important,
You don't need to call me back."
You were referring to your life.
I knew that, by the laws of shadow.
Later. Fine, you said.
Why did I decide to murder you?

Out of control, you released your demons.
Even they were generous, not jealous.
What is it that you did?
I let the night slip away. I don't know why.
Now, there is nothing and no one to forgive.

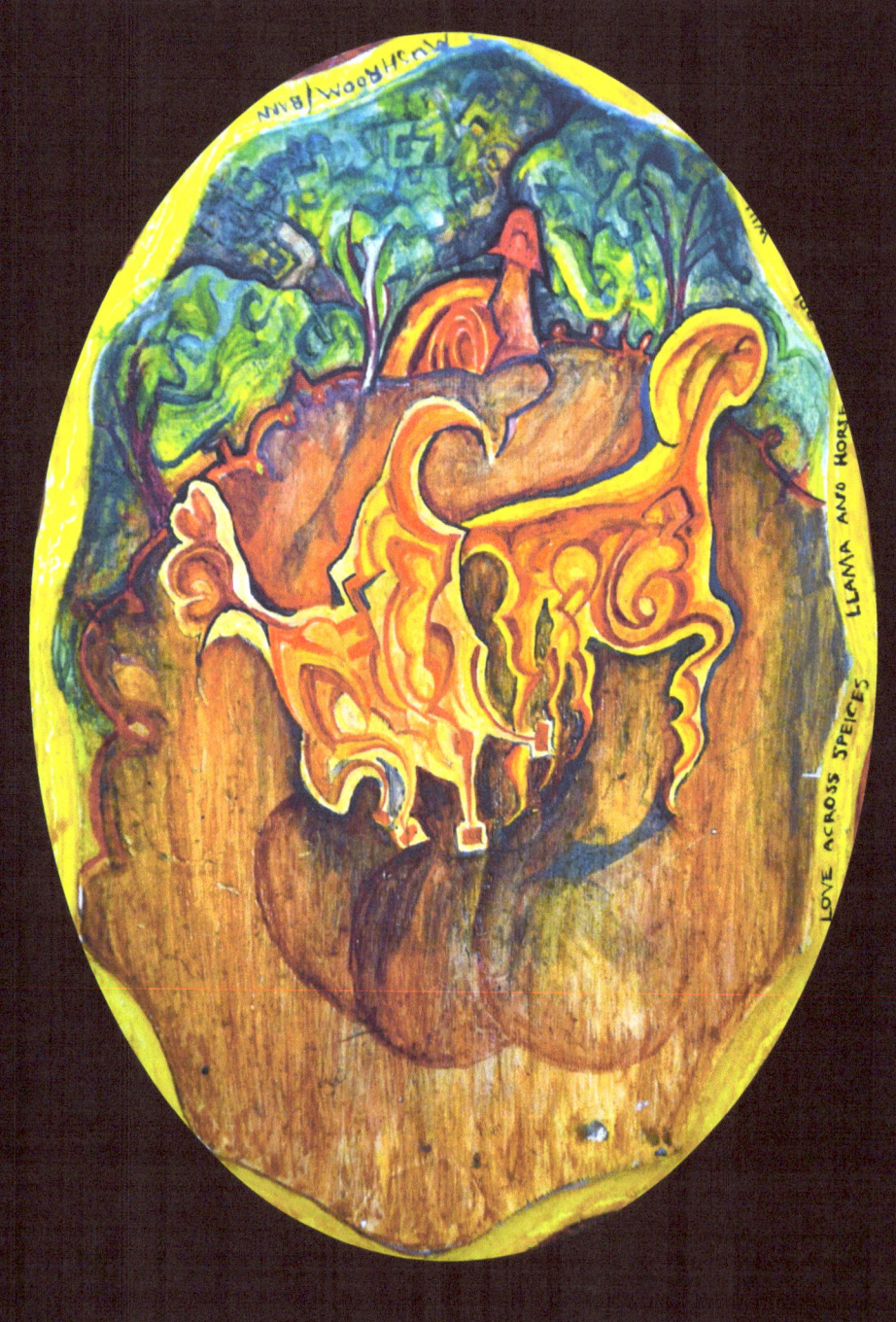

HORSE AND A LLAMA 6.5X9.5" (17X24 CM), OIL ON WOOD, 2002

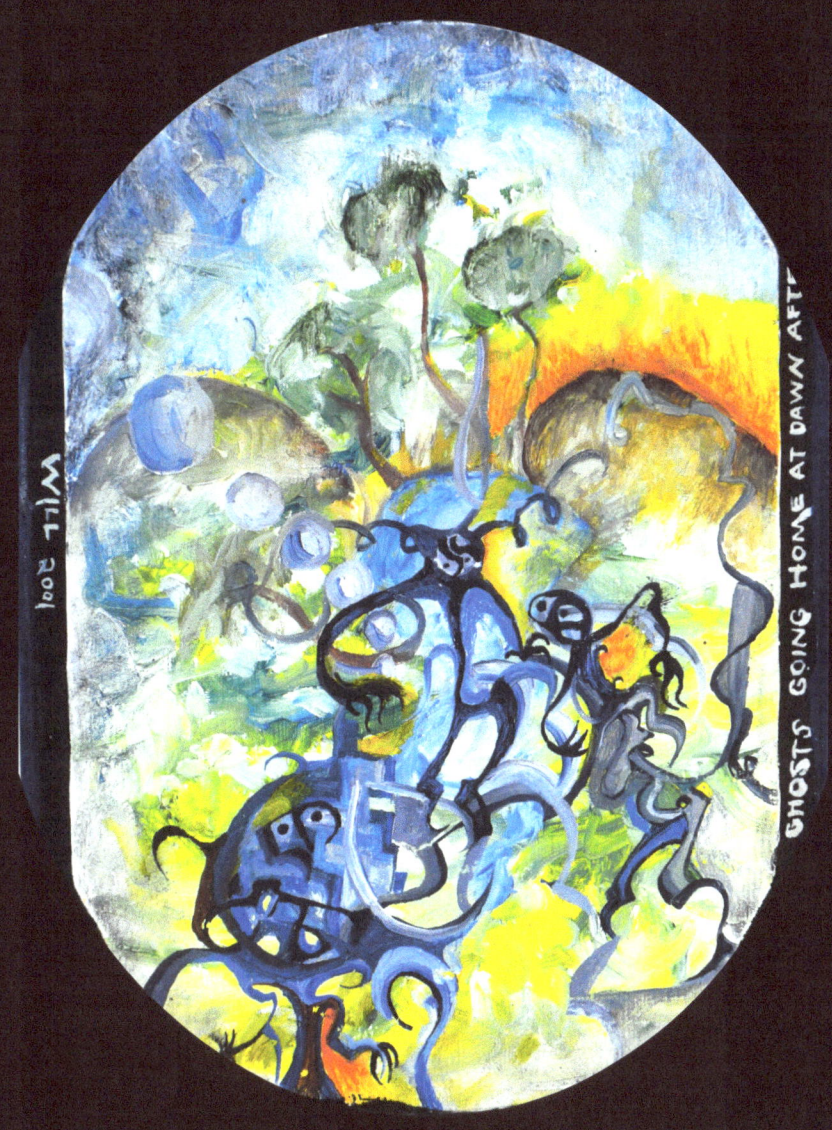

GHOSTS GOING HOME AT DAWN 6.5X9.5" (17X24 CM), OIL ON WOOD, 2002

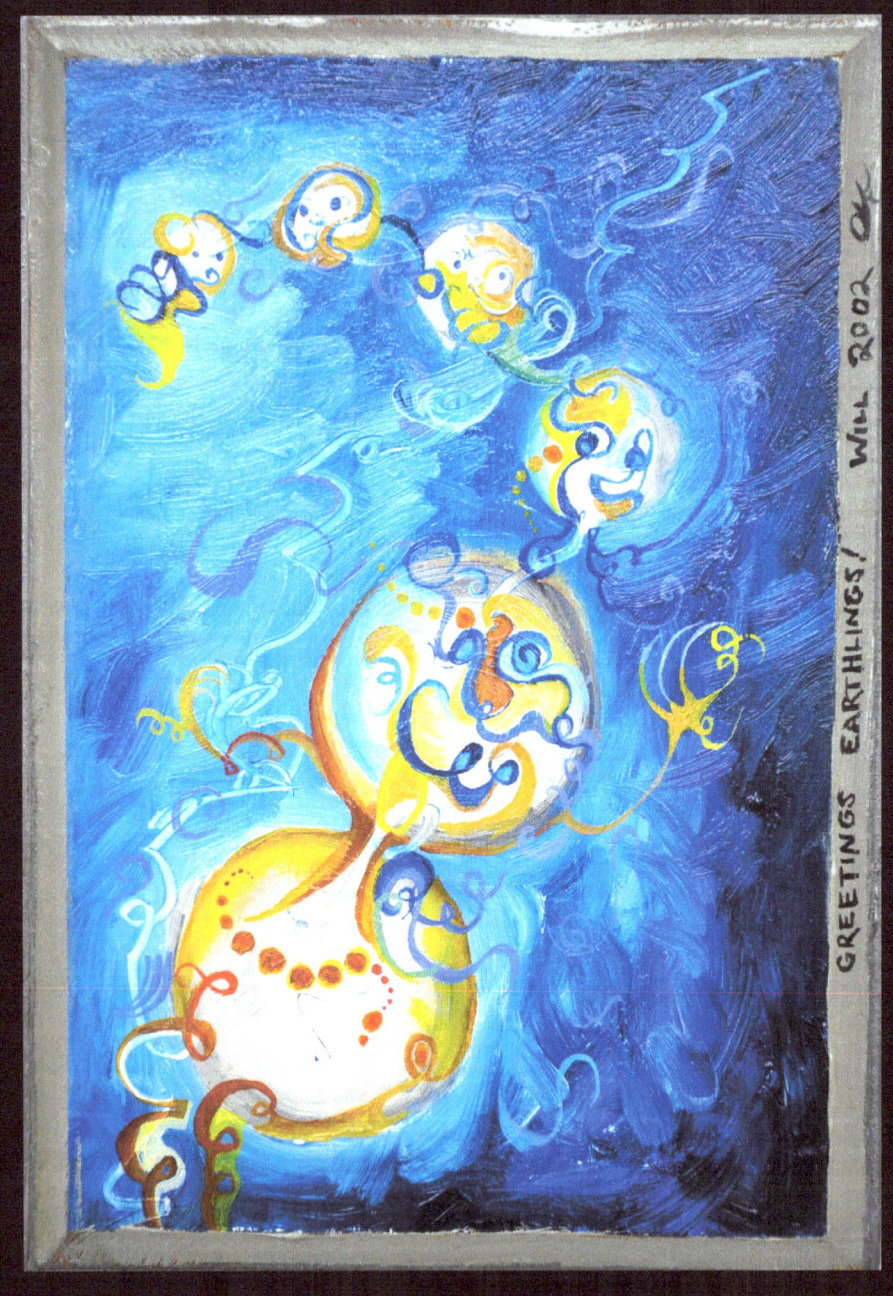

GREETINGS EARTHLINGS 6.5X9.5" (17X24 CM), OIL ON WOOD, 2002

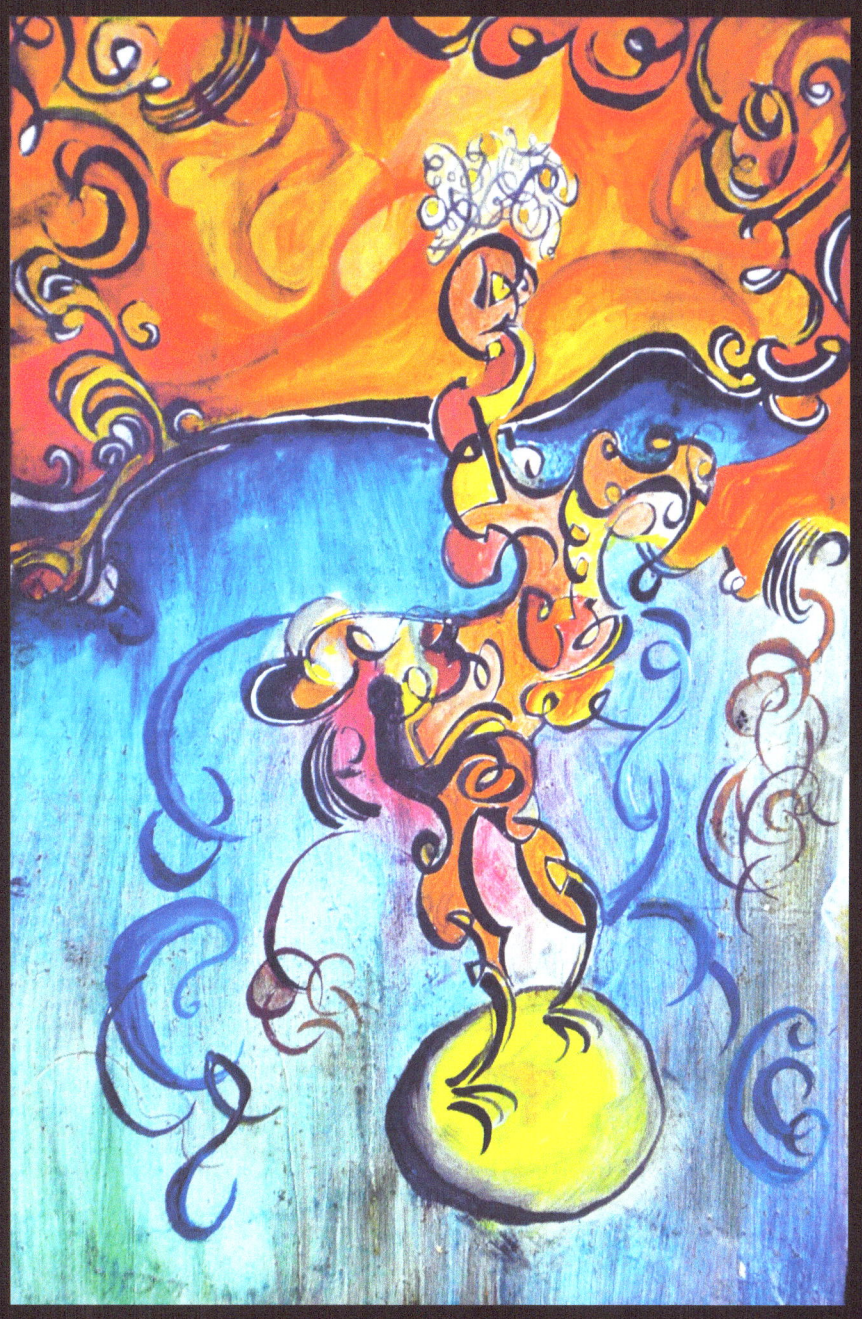

ROOSTING ON HER EGG 6.5X9.5" (17X24 CM), OIL ON WOOD, 2002

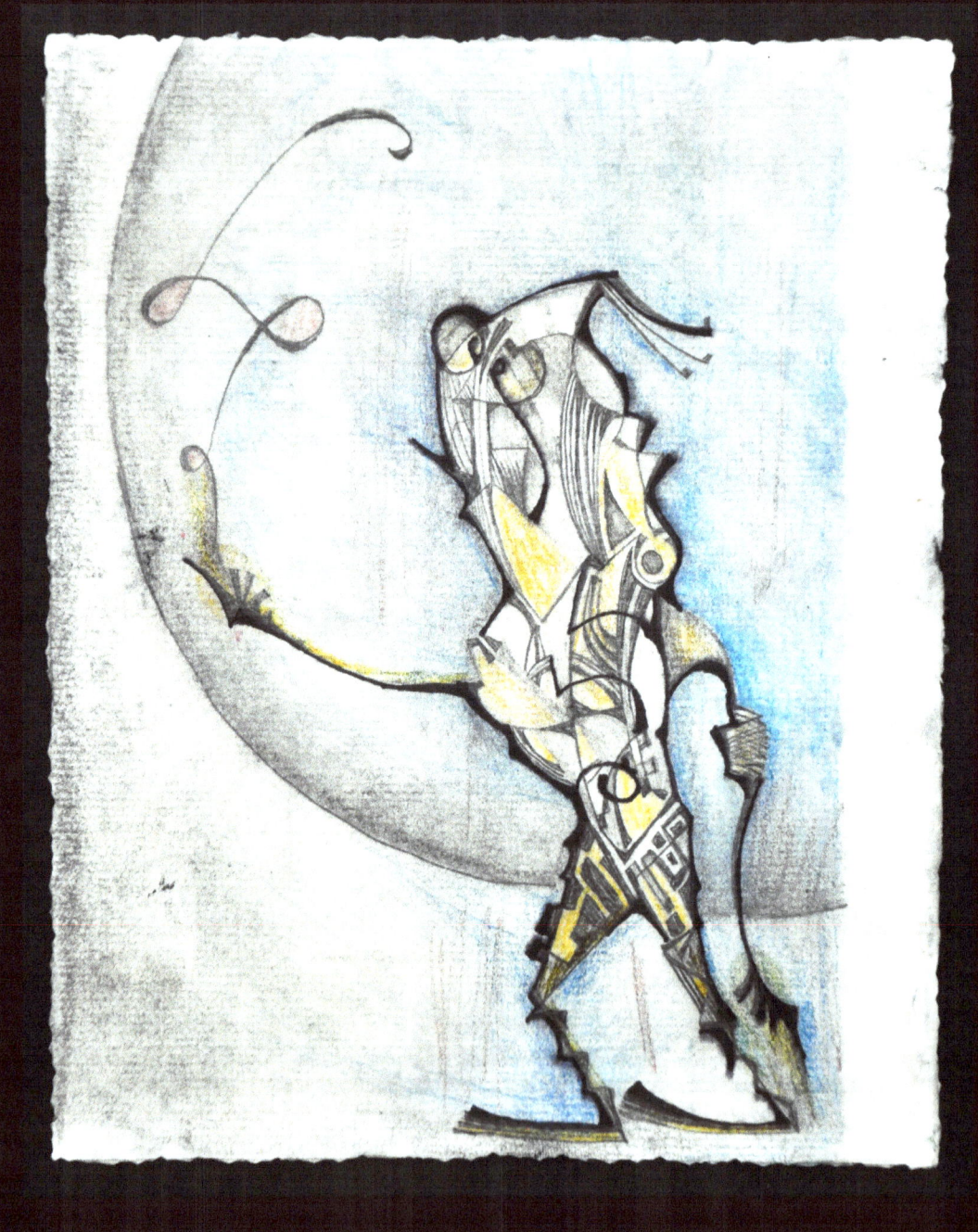

HERE GOES NOTHING 7.5X8.5" (19X22 CM), INK AND WATERCOLOR ON PAPER, 2004

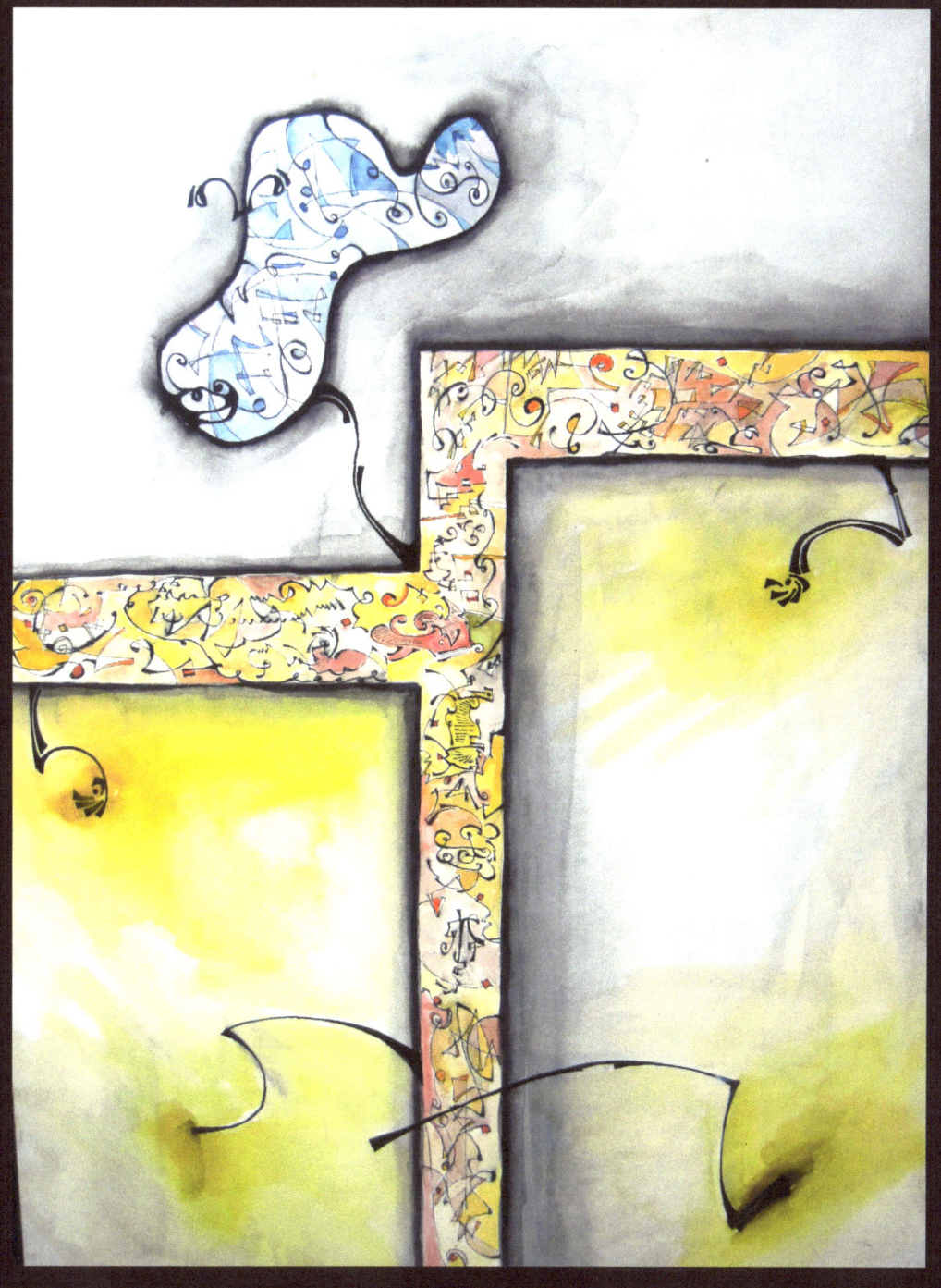

STICK MAN 12x16" (30x41 CM), INK AND WATERCOLOR ON PAPER, 1997

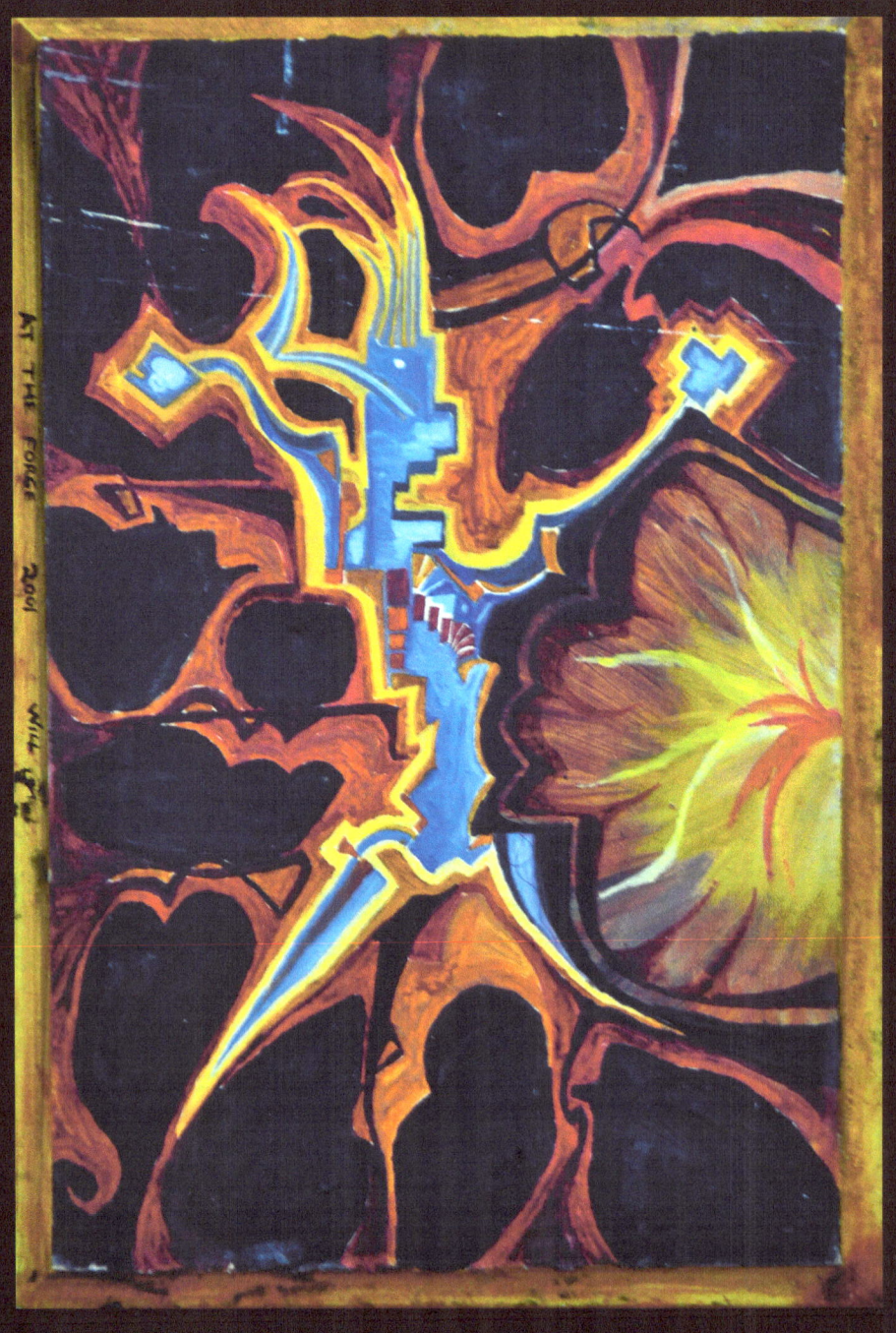

AT THE FORGE 6.5X9.5" (17X24 CM), OIL ON WOOD, 2001

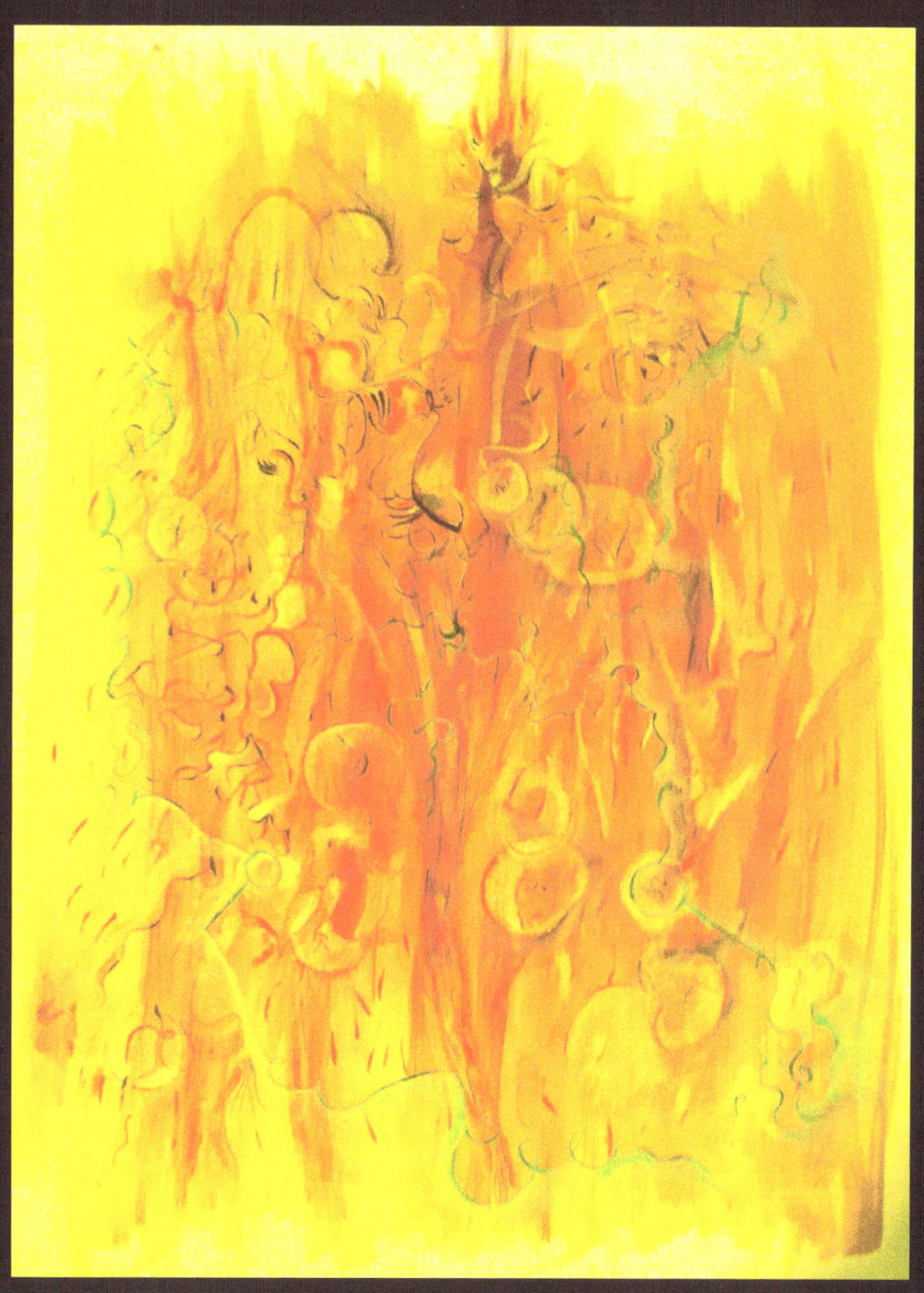

WALKING ON TIGHT ROPE OVER THICKET 16.5x22" (42x56 CM), OIL ON PAPER, 2013